UFC®

ULTIMATE FIGHTING® CHAMPIONSHIP®

OFFICIAL FAN'S GUIDE

First published in 2011 by Carlton Books
Reprinted with updates in 2014

Carlton Books Limited
20 Mortimer Street
London W1T 3JW

ISBN: 978-1-78097-547-4

Project art editor: Luke Griffin
Designer: Ben Ruocco
Production: Maria Petalidou
Editorial: Nicky Gyopari and Lesley Levene
Project editors: Matt Lowing and Martin Corteel

Printed and bound in China

Anthony B Evans attended his first UFC event in 2002, and has been covering combat sports all his professional life. A writer and publicist, he has worked for as varied publications as *Boxing Monthly*, *Fighters Only*, *Boxing News*, *The Sun*, the *Sydney Telegraph*, and UFC.com.

Thomas Gerbasi is the Editorial Director for the Ultimate Fighting Championship and has written on combat sports for various publications for over a decade. An award-winning member of the Boxing Writers Association of America, his work has also appeared in *The Independent*, *YahooSports.com*, *ESPN.com*, *MSNCanada*, *Inked*, and *KING* magazine.

UFC

ULTIMATE FIGHTING CHAMPIONSHIP

OFFICIAL FAN'S GUIDE

AS REAL AS IT GETS

With forewords by **Dana White, UFC President**
and **Michael Bisping, UFC Middleweight**

CARLTON
BOOKS

CONTENTS

FOREWORD

In the history of the Ultimate Fighting Championship, there have been more twists and turns than I care to remember. While the sport has grown incredibly over the past few years and we're finally seeing the growth that we always believed in, the UFC wasn't always packing more than 55,000 people into stadiums as we did at UFC 129 in Toronto.

If there is one thing that has always been consistent, it's that we have loyal fans that spread the word about fights and fighters. They make sure that all their friends and family members know the excitement of mixed martial arts.

That kind of loyalty is rare these days. Without the fans, we wouldn't be here today. When you read through this book, I hope you're able to relive some of the UFC's greatest moments, see how far we've come and perhaps discover new things about the sport.

While we're continually evolving and making this bigger and better, I hope that this *UFC Official Fan's Guide* is something that marks this first generation in UFC history.

Thanks for the support throughout the years, and I hope you enjoy the book.

Dana White
UFC President

FOREWORD

When I began training in martial arts as a kid, the UFC didn't even exist, and competing in front of packed arenas and international TV cameras was the stuff of fantasies.

In 2003 I took a huge gamble, as a young father with bills to pay, on the emerging sport of mixed martial arts, and in December 2005, I tried out for *The Ultimate Fighter®*. My life changed forever.

Winning *TUF* and fighting in the UFC have enabled me to provide for my family, see the world, and meet some incredible people. It is still weird for me to see action figures and posters of myself or to see tens of thousands of fans pack the biggest arenas in the world.

But as big as the UFC is now compared to the pipe dream of competing in martial arts for a living when I was younger, this is just the beginning for the UFC. I honestly believe mixed martial arts is the most exciting sport in the world and, by the time my kids are grown up, the UFC will have taken its place alongside the World Cup and Super Bowl as the biggest sports events on the planet.

Michael Bisping
UFC Middleweight

INTRODUCTION

November 1993. To most of the world, boxing was still king, but to a few innovative souls who thought that it was time for a little shakeup on the combat sports scene, things were about to change forever. The moment a young man from Brazil named Royce Gracie stepped into an eight-sided cage dubbed "The Octagon®," suddenly everything that came before didn't seem as important or compelling.

That fall night in Denver, Colorado, Gracie introduced Brazilian Jiu-Jitsu (BJJ) into the mainstream world's consciousness, and a sport—mixed martial arts (MMA)—was born.

For fans like us, those early days were captivating simply because of the Wild West feel to the proceedings—600lb Emmanuel Yarborough fighting Keith Hackney, Gracie submitting Art Jimmerson, who wore one boxing glove in their match, and Tank Abbott running through opponents with an attitude and knockout power.

But eventually, as MMA evolved, it was necessary to take everything to the next level. New owners arrived in 2001, and when the Fertitta brothers and Dana White entered the picture, they made a concerted effort to get the sport sanctioned around the United States and the world while marketing the then-dying brand not as a spectacle, but as a sport, and the fighters as true professional athletes, which they were.

Since then, the world has caught on to what a handful of us knew back in 1993—that this is the greatest sport in the world, a true proving ground for athletes willing to test themselves in a one-on-one environment with only their wits, fists, and feet to protect them.

And this book is for you. Whether you're an old-school fight junkie, a newcomer to the sport, or somewhere in between, there's something in here for every fan of the Ultimate Fighting Championship, and we just hope we've done the sport justice in the pages that follow.

**Anthony B Evans &
Thomas Gerbasi**

THE STORY OF THE UFC®

It was supposed to be a one-off, a sideshow. And yet the UFC rapidly evolved into one of the biggest sports organizations on earth. This is the remarkable story of the UFC so far...

The UFC Octagon—the sport's ultimate proving ground. Sam Stout celebrates after knocking out Yves Edwards at UFC 131.

HOW IT ALL BEGAN

The first Ultimate Fighting Championship event may have taken place as recently as the early 1990s, but the sport now known as mixed martial arts still has a rich history spanning several centuries.

Ken Shamrock leg-locks Patrick Smith at UFC 1.

Although UFC brought mixed martial arts (MMA) crashing into the public consciousness as recently as 1993, the idea of taking the most effective aspects of striking and grappling and mixing them together into a single combative art is not a new one. The idea first occurred to the ancient Greeks, who dubbed the combination of boxing and wrestling "Pankration" and introduced it to the Olympic Games in 648 BC.

However, just as boxing died out as an art until it was revitalized in the 18th century, it was eons before anything resembling MMA would be seen again.

One of the most important figures in the history of MMA's modern "rebirth" was Mitsuyo Maeda, a Japanese prizefighter who was born in 1878.

As with so many fighters of the time, we will never know if Maeda truly defeated 2,000 opponents in no-holds-barred contests, as the legend would have us believe. But what is clear—even through the mists of time—is that Maeda was a legitimate fighter with some serious skills.

Maeda eventually settled in Brazil and there he passed on his distinctive form of judo to one Carlos Gracie, who, in turn, changed and adapted the art along with his brothers.

But it was the frail, sickly younger brother Hélio who adapted the art still further into a fighting system that would forever change the way in which martial arts was viewed worldwide. Hélio lacked the physical strength to perform many of the techniques his brothers had perfected and reconstructed the art so that patience and leverage were more important than aggression and raw power.

"Gracie jiu-jitsu"—or Brazilian Jiu-Jitsu (BJJ)—was born and Hélio and the brothers became legends in their native Brazil by accepting Vale Tudo ("anything goes") challenges from anyone from boxing, wrestling, or martial arts.

"If you want your face beaten and well smashed and your arms broken, contact Carlos Gracie at this address."

And with that newspaper ad in the 1920s, the family laid down a gauntlet for all those who questioned the effectiveness of Gracie jiu-jitsu in a real fight. Even legendary heavyweight boxing champion Joe Louis got an invite when at the height of his powers in the 1940s, one that he never responded to.

And those who did respond to the ad got a lesson they would not soon forget, usually from Hélio, who won challenge match after challenge match against fighters from different combat sports disciplines over the years in bouts that captured the imagination of the public.

By 1951, these matches had gained national attention, with Gracie's bout against Japan's Masahiko Kimura drawing 120,000 people to Maracana Stadium in Brazil. The Gracies were national celebrities, even garnering television shows such as *Vale Tudo* on TV and *Heroes of the Ring*.

But the American market was tougher to crack, until 1991, when California advertising executive Art Davie publicized a videotape entitled "Gracies in Action" which featured the family's challenge matches.

U.S. martial arts aficionados loved it. Sales of the tape went through the roof, and Davie and Hélio's son Rorion came up with the idea of putting together an event pitting fighters of different martial arts styles against each other in a tournament format to determine which style was best.

Thankfully, ideas such as having the fighters compete while surrounded by crocodiles were left on the drawing board, and the promoters secured funding for a concept of a one-night, single-elimination tournament which they were originally going to call "War of the Worlds."

However, by the time the event took place at a packed McNichols Arena in Denver, Colorado, on November 12, 1993, it was the "Ultimate Fighting Championship" which completely revolutionized the way the world viewed fighting.

The event was billed as no-holds-barred. It featured an eight-man tournament in which the winner would need to defeat three opponents to win the $50,000 first prize. The contestants included boxer Art Jimmerson, sumo fighter Teila Tuli, taekwondo champion and boxer Patrick Smith, kickboxers Kevin Rosier, Gerard Gordeau, Zane Frazier, and "shooter" pro wrestler Ken Shamrock.

In an echo of yesteryear, the family selected Royce Gracie, the youngest and most unintimidating of Hélio's sons, to represent the family honor.

Royce defeated Jimmerson, Shamrock and Gordeau by submission easily, obliterating such myths as boxing is "real fighting," huge muscles are needed to fight and if you are on your back, you must be getting beaten up.

Not only was a star born that night, so was a sport, now known as mixed marial arts.

Bare knuckles and crude attacks were the order of the day at the early UFC bouts.

THE NEXT CHAPTER

The supposedly "one-off" UFC event was a huge success on American Pay-Per-View and home video worldwide, so the early promoters organized a sequel. And another. And another… creating a brand-new sport without realizing it.

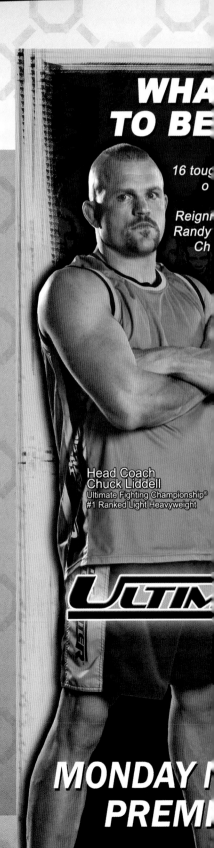

WHA
TO BE

16 toug
o

Reign
Randy
Ch

Head Coach
Chuck Liddell
Ultimate Fighting Championship®
#1 Ranked Light Heavyweight

ULTIM

The original UFC promoters—known as SEG—had a hit on their hands but opted to aim for the lowest common denominator. Believing the UFC had a limited shelf life, they promoted the sport with such banal sloganeering as "Two Men Enter… One Man Leaves," and as a spectacle, not a sport.

Inevitably, the events began to encounter resistance from local media and politicians, until Senator John McCain, the same man who had introduced the "Ali Act" in an attempt to clean up boxing and would eventually run for President of the United States, made it his mission to destroy the UFC.

In a situation entirely of their own making the UFC's owners now struggled to find places to put on fights, and even to pay fighters' purses, and began losing top talent to the Japanese MMA promotion PRIDE FC. Then, when the UFC was thrown off Pay-Per-View under the weight of McCain's protests, the future looked very bleak indeed.

It was during his December 2000 negotiations for his fighter Chuck Liddell that a fight manager named Dana White learned just how dire things had gotten for the organization. White recalled: "I was negotiating for the fight and they said 'Look, we got no money and we don't even know if we will be in business much longer.'"

White telephoned his friend and casino owner Lorenzo Fertitta, who, along with elder brother Frank, was a BJJ practitioner and huge MMA fan. Within a month, the three owned the UFC and their parent company Zuffa (Italian for "Fight") began the process of representing the UFC as a sport.

White knew it would be a long process but under his leadership the successes began to dribble in: Nevada agreed to sanction the sport, enabling the UFC to finally put on shows in the fight capital of the world. Then UFC 40, featuring the first grudge match between Tito Ortiz and Ken Shamrock, showed early signs that the fans would return for certain matches.

But while there were signs of growth, it was all coming too slow. Zuffa was bleeding money and there was a morning when Lorenzo telephoned White and told him to sell the company, only to change his mind hours later.

White said he had his moments of doubt, too. "I always believed the UFC could be the biggest sport on earth, but there were days when I thought maybe we had the right idea but at the wrong time."

The final throw of the dice for Zuffa

The nuclear-hot feud between Ken Shamrock and Tito Ortiz resulted in UFC 40 drawing what was then a record audience.

MONDAY
PREMI

came when the company paid over $10 million to produce a reality TV series it placed on Spike TV called *The Ultimate Fighter*. The format—almost immediately copied by boxing—featured two teams of promising but unsigned fighters living together, training together, and competing against each other to win a six-figure UFC contract. UFC legends Randy Couture and Chuck Liddell—who were set to face off months later—were the ideal two personalities to serve as coaches. "*TUF*," as it became known, debuted in January of 2005 and everything changed.

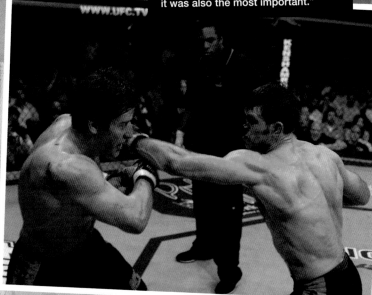

Dana White: "The first Forrest Griffin vs. Stephan Bonnar fight was not only one of the best fights in UFC history, it was also the most important."

OES IT TAKE REAL FIGHTER?

competitors are about to find
kes to be a UFC fighter!

ight Heavyweight Champion,
nd the Sport's #1 Contender,
lead their teams in an all
ar to see who is...

Head Coach
Randy Couture
Ultimate Fighting Championship®
World Light Heavyweight Champ

THE **TE FIGHTER**

Spike™
NETWORK FOR MEN

NTS AT 11 PM ET/PT
ES JANUARY 17TH

"That was the Trojan Horse," White said. "People watched that show who would never, ever have dreamed of otherwise watching a fight. But with *TUF* they got to see how hard these guys train, what great athletes and people they are, and suddenly they got it. They got what a great sport this is."

But while the series did well, what really ushered in a new dawn for the UFC was, of course, a fight.

Forrest Griffin and Stephan Bonnar had reached the finale of the series and faced off on live TV to win the six-figure contract. Both men threw everything and anything they had at the other in a 15-minute fight which perhaps will never be eclipsed in terms of drama.

Fans began to telephone and email their friends, telling them they HAD to tune in. After 15 minutes, Griffin was given the decision but Zuffa awarded both men a contract.

Months later, *UFC 52: Liddell v Couture II*, shattered all previous company records for a Pay-Per-View.

The modern era of the UFC—and the fastest rise of any sports organization or any sport, period—was about to take the world by storm.

White said: "*The Ultimate Fighter* series—and that fight in the finale between Griffin and Bonnar—is what saved the UFC."

Even McCain was impressed: "Many years ago I spoke out against Ultimate Fighting," he said in 2007. "But the sport has grown up... it focuses on integrity and its many fans deserve no less."

The original magazine ad for the very first series of *The Ultimate Fighter*.

THE MAINSTREAM

After the success of *The Ultimate Fighter*, the UFC began to make a rapid ascension to the sorts of heights even the most ardent of fans would never have dared predict just a year previously...

In the years following *TUF I*, the UFC's popularity exploded worldwide. While traditional combat sports had largely failed to make an impression on younger fans, the UFC became the destination of choice for a new generation of fight fans.

A whole lifestyle sprang up around the UFC, and martial arts became more popular across the world than at any point since the karate/kung-fu craze of the 1970s.

There was a time UFC events were not even released on home video, but now fans had the chance to wear UFC shirts and hoodies, go to the gym, and use UFC equipment, or even go to an official UFC Gym, grab a UFC action figure, or play one of the official UFC video games. Even Hollywood began to cast UFC champions like Georges St-Pierre and Ronda Rousey in A-list blockbusters.

"I always believed the UFC could become as big as this," said UFC President Dana White. "But, when people tell me we are now mainstream, I always say we have barely scratched the surface. Right now, we are in half a billion homes worldwide. Wait until we are in a billion homes.

A front-kick is a rare but effective striking technique, as demonstrated by Mike Pyle on Jesse Lennox at UFC 115.

This is just getting started; we still have a lot of work to do before we are mainstream. The Super Bowl, the World Cup, that's mainstream and that's where we want to be in the next five, 10 years and we are going to bust our asses to get there."

While the UFC continues to set record television ratings, live gate attendances and Pay-Per-View buy-rates, one of the continued frustrations for the UFC—and its fans—is that the state of New York will not sanction professional MMA.

White said: "I've given up saying when we will be in New York. I said last year, I said the year before. Now I'm just saying that we will get it done; I'm not predicting anything other than that. We are in every State in the U.S. and all over North America. It's insane we aren't in New York."

But the UFC hasn't concentrated all its efforts on the U.S. White always believed in the UFC's global appeal, and the company always had plans to take the sport across the globe. In early 2007, its one-time rival, PRIDE, was bought out by Zuffa, setting up a series of dream fights between PRIDE legends such as Wanderlei Silva and the UFC's Chuck Liddell, as well as the historic unification of the UFC and PRIDE 205-pound and 185-pound championships.

UFC offices were opened in London, Toronto and Beijing, and agencies were hired across the world from Brazil to Mexico, from the United Arab Emirates to Japan to Australia. The UFC dominated world's box offices like no live event since the Rolling Stones's heyday, selling out the world's most prestigious venues on five continents. UFC programming can now be seen in more than 140 countries, in 19 languages. Local versions of The Ultimate Fighter have been produced for Brazil, the UK, Australia, Canada and Asia, and a UFC television channel was launched across Latin America.

On March 12, 2011, the UFC announced it had purchased Strikeforce, an MMA organization that had a loyal following in the U.S. All the world's best fighters were finally under one promotional banner, and the UFC added lower weight classes and a 135-pound women's division that captured the imagination of fans all over the world.

"We are going to continue to put on the best fights between the best fighters," said White. "We listen to our fans and give them the fights they want to see. That's our job—put on fights the fans want to see—and it's the best job in the world.

"I get asked in interviews: 'What is your exit strategy? Is it when the UFC does a stadium or makes this much money or you do this event or that deal?' No, none of that. Lorenzo, Frank, and me have got no exit strategy. We are not going anywhere."

Great Britain's Dan Hardy refuses to submit to Georges St-Pierre's armbar at UFC 111.

EXPLAINED

Once seen by the uninformed as a crude blood sport with no holds barred, mixed martial arts is, in reality, a professional sport with many rules and regulations to protect the athletes while they're competing.

Bout Duration

- All non-championship bouts shall be three rounds.
- All championship bouts shall be five rounds.
- Rounds will be five minutes in duration.
- A one-minute rest period will occur between each round.

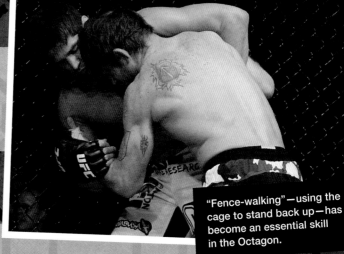

"Fence-walking"—using the cage to stand back up—has become an essential skill in the Octagon.

Fouls

- Butting with the head.
- Eye gouging of any kind.
- Biting.
- Hair pulling.
- Fish hooking.
- Groin attacks of any kind.
- Putting a finger into any orifice or into any cut or laceration on an opponent.
- Small joint manipulation.
- Striking to the spine or the back of the head.
- Striking downward using the point of the elbow.
- Throat strikes of any kind, including, without limitation, grabbing the trachea.
- Clawing, pinching, or twisting of the flesh.
- Grabbing the clavicle.
- Kicking the head of a grounded opponent.
- Kneeing the head of a grounded opponent.
- Stomping a grounded opponent.
- Kicking to the kidney with the heel.
- Spiking an opponent to the canvas on his head or neck.
- Throwing an opponent out of the ring or fenced area.
- Holding the shorts or gloves of an opponent.
- Spitting at an opponent.
- Engaging in unsportsmanlike conduct that causes injury to an opponent.
- Holding the ropes or the fence.
- Using abusive language in the ring or fenced area.
- Attacking an opponent on or during the break.
- Attacking an opponent who is under the care of the referee.
- Attacking an opponent after the bell has sounded the end of the period of unarmed combat.
- Flagrantly disregarding the instructions of the referee.
- Timidity, including, but without limitation, avoiding contact with an opponent, intentionally or consistently dropping the mouthpiece, or faking an injury.
- Interference by the corner.
- Throwing in the towel during competition.

Ways to Win

- Submission by:
  - Physical tap out.
  - Verbal tap out.
- Technical knockout by the referee stopping the contest.
- Decision via scorecards, including:
  - Unanimous decision:
  All judges pick the same fighter as the winner.
  - Split decision:
  One judge picks one fighter, the other two judges pick the other fighter.
  - Majority decision:
  Two of the three judges pick the same fighter as the winner, the final judge says the fight was a draw.
  - Draw:
  Unanimous draw.
  Majority draw.
  Split draw.
- Technical decision.
- Technical draw.
- Disqualification.
- Forfeit.
- No contest.
Referee may restart the round:
If the fighters reach a stalemate and do not work to improve position or finish.

The most exciting sport in the world packs another arena. This time it is Bell Centre, Montreal, for UFC 83.

Styles

Boxing
The skill or sport of fighting with the fists, usually with padded leather gloves. Referred to as the "sweet science," boxers use elaborate foot maneuvers and quick jabs for offense.

Brazilian Jiu-Jitsu
In the mid-1920s, Carlos Gracie opened the Gracie Jiu-Jitsu Academy in Rio de Janeiro, Brazil. He taught the skills he learned from Japanese Judo master Esai Maeda. The skills were later modified to use less strength and to be more effective against larger opponents. Brazilian Jiu-Jitsu's reputation spread due to the success of its practitioners in no-holds-barred contests.

Jiu-jitsu
Ancient Japanese martial art that encompasses throwing, joint locks, striking, and weapons training.

Judo
Sportive Japanese martial art founded in 1882 by Jigoro Kano. Derived from jiu-jitsu, judo is now an Olympic sport that emphasizes throws. Striking is not allowed in competition Judo.

Karate
Name used to identify many Japanese and Okinawan martial arts. While known for powerful, linear techniques, many karate styles also incorporate softer, circular techniques. Some of the popular styles of karate are Kyokushinkai, Shotokan, Goju-Ryu, Shorin-Ryu, and Kenpo, which was the first "Americanized" version of karate.

Kickboxing
Sportive martial art combining boxing punches and martial arts kicks. Many different styles with different rules exist, such as Muay Thai, Full Contact Karate, and Asian Rules Fighting.

Kung Fu
Also referred to as Gung Fu, Chinese Boxing, and Wu Shu. There are hundreds of kung fu styles. Many are patterned after the movements of animals. Some well-known styles of kung fu are Wing Chun, Praying Mantis, Pau Kua, Tai-Chi-Ch'uan, and Shuai Chiao.

Taekwondo
One of the most practiced martial arts in the world, taekwondo is a Korean style known for its flashy kicking techniques.

Wrestling
Possibly the world's oldest sport. Contestants struggle hand to hand, attempting to throw or take down their opponent without striking blows. Some of the many styles of wrestling are Freestyle, Greco-Roman, and catch as catch can.

THE OCTAGON

"We can settle this in the Octagon" has become part of the modern lexicon. The UFC's trademarked eight-sided fenced structure has replaced boxing's squared circle as combat sport's ultimate proving ground. It is a place of ultimate truth, where the pre-fight boasts count for nothing and respect sells itself dearly.

When the group who came up with the idea for a one-night, single-elimination tournament called the Ultimate Fighting Championship first talked about what the fighting area should be, they faced a conundrum. There is a technique in boxing and kickboxing known as "cutting off the ring," which involves a subtle use of footwork to trap an opponent in the corner. It takes years to master and clearly would give fighters from these backgrounds an advantage.

So, somehow, the group stumbled toward the idea of an eight-sided surface, fenced off to ensure fighters could not fall to the arena floor, as sometimes happens in sumo. Thank goodness the idea of a cage surrounded by crocodiles was laughed off.

Today, the UFC Octagon is unique in all of sport and is inherently associated with the UFC brand. To fighters from around the world, it represents the pinnacle of their craft: to fight in the Octagon is, to a mixed martial artist, the same as playing in the World Cup for a soccer player or running in the Olympic Games for a sprinter.

To fans, the Octagon is the theater of the impossible, where larger-than-life heroes collide and legends are forged.

HEIGHT FROM CANVAS TO TOP OF FENCE:
5ft 9in (1.7m)

OCTAGON FACTS:
- Each canvas is used only once.

- There are actually five Octagons, three in the US, one in Europe, and one in Australia.

- UFC production crews need at least 14 hours to "load in" the Octagon and lighting rig.

- The UFC 80 Octagon canvas, on which he finally won the UFC lightweight belt, hangs in BJ Penn's private gym in Hawaii.

WALKWAY:
4ft (1.2m) wide,
4ft (1.2m) high

ENTRANCE GATES:
Two on opposite sides of Octagon, each 3ft (0.9m) wide, 5ft (1.5m) high

INTERIOR:
(Fighting space)
30ft (9m) across

HEIGHT FROM GROUND TO CANVAS:
4ft (1.2m)

EXTERIOR:
38ft (11.6m) in diameter

TOP 10 *UFC*
KNOCKOUTS OF ALL TIME

Few endings in sport captivate an audience like a knockout. Think of it as a home run, touchdown, and goal all rolled up into one. And when you're talking about spectacular finishes, the UFC is the place to be.

Rashad Evans KO2 Chuck Liddell

UFC 88 A month after Rashad Evans' 2007 win over Michael Bisping in the main event of UFC 78, former UFC light heavyweight champion Chuck Liddell broke a two-fight losing streak with a big victory over longtime nemesis Wanderlei Silva. The victory reestablished Liddell in the 205lb pecking order, while Evans was still seen as the upstart who was about to be sent back down the ladder by "The Iceman" when the two stepped into the Octagon at UFC 88 in September of 2008. But Evans, now showing his fight-ending power combined with his world-class fighting IQ, frustrated Liddell throughout the first round with his movement and rapid-fire flurries, and when Liddell got overaggressive in round two, Evans closed the show with a single punch, silencing a raucous Atlanta crowd and propelling "Suga" on his way to a world title shot that he made good on when he defeated Forrest Griffin.

Rashad Evans' fastball right hand on Chuck Liddell at UFC 88 was one of the most spectacular one-punch KOs ever.

Chuck Liddell's right hand earned him a revenge win over Randy Couture.

UFC 52 It was fast—only 2:06—but in winning the UFC light heavyweight title after close to seven years in the fight game, Chuck Liddell finally had the validation all fighters hope to one day get as he knocked out Randy Couture with a right hand at UFC 52 in April of 2005. Sure Liddell said all the right things throughout the years, insisting that he would fight even without the belt on the line, but at the end of the day, every fighter wants to be a champion, and when "The Iceman" finally got to the top, and by knockout against a fighter who stopped him two years earlier, no less, that was redemption. The two UFC Hall of Famers would meet one more time, at UFC 57 in February of 2006, and the result was the same as the second bout—Liddell by knockout.

"I want to beat everyone who's beaten me, this was very satisfying." Chuck Liddell

Tank Abbott KO1 Steve Nelmark

UFC 11.5 When UFC fans think of David "Tank" Abbott, the first things that usually come to mind are the devastating knockouts he delivered in the early days of the UFC against the likes of John Matua and Paul Varelans. And though he wasn't the most technical fighter to set foot in the Octagon, Abbott's brawling style left an indelible mark in the UFC history books and especially on the recipient of his most devastating knockout—Steve Nelmark. Stalking Nelmark with his hands down by his side in the 1996 bout on the Ultimate Ultimate card, Tank got a hold of his opponent, slammed him to the mat, and after surviving a brief guillotine choke attempt, he unleashed a barrage of strikes, with a final right hand leaving Nelmark twisted and defeated on the mat. Surprisingly, it would be another year before Abbott scored another win, a 1997 decision over Yoji Anjo.

Vitor Belfort TKO1 Wanderlei Silva

Vitor Belfort stuns Wanderlei Silva at the original UFC Brazil, October 16, 1998.

UFC 17.5 With countrymen Vitor "The Phenom" Belfort and Wanderlei "The Axe Murderer" Silva both possessing the ability to end a fight in an instant, you just knew that their fight at UFC Ultimate Brazil in October of 1998 was going to end explosively. Well, it did, with the 21-year-old Belfort stopping his local rival with a dazzling array of strikes just 44 seconds into the first round that sent the Sao Paulo crowd into a frenzy. Silva, just two years into his career at the time, would soon go on to greatness in Japan. For Belfort, 6-1 at the time and on top of his game, it was to be his last UFC bout for three years, as he proceeded to sign a deal with PRIDE in Japan that saw him win four of five fights from 1999 to 2001, with his only loss coming to the legendary Kazushi Sakuraba.

Anderson Silva KO1 Vitor Belfort

"The Spider" celebrates the first leaping front-kick KO in UFC history.

UFC 126 Widely considered to be the most dangerous threat to Anderson Silva's UFC middleweight title reign, explosive veteran Vitor Belfort had the style and experience to test "The Spider," and he had every intention of doing so. But when faced with such a threat, Silva did what you're supposed to do—eliminate it immediately—as he knocked out "The Phenom" in the first round of their UFC 126 bout in February of 2011, ending matters for all intents and purposes with a spectacular front-kick to the chin that the champion claimed was taught to him by martial arts film star Steven Seagal. "That's just one of the tricks I was working on," said Silva, who retained his crown for the eighth time, breaking a tie with Matt Hughes for most successful title defenses in UFC history.

"This is just one of the tricks we have been working on in the gym!"
Anderson Silva

Gary Goodridge KO1 Paul Herrera

Goodridge slams home a series of elbows to take UFC 8 KO win.

UFC 8 In February of 1996, Kuk Sool Won practitioner Gary Goodridge entered the Octagon for the first time, wearing a traditional gi, and he proceeded to make one of the most memorable debuts in UFC history against Paul Herrera at UFC 8. Taking just 13 seconds to finish the bout, Goodridge made Herrera pay for what he believed was some pre-fight trash talk and after locking his foe in an inescapable crucifix position, what followed was a frightening series of elbows that knocked Herrera out and began the legend of the man known internationally as "Big Daddy." And what a career it was for Goodridge, who followed his UFC success with a long run in the PRIDE organization in Japan. Yet no matter what else he did, everyone always referred back to that first knockout win.

"The rules are you keep hitting until the ref says stop."
Gary Goodridge

Anderson Silva dominates Rich Franklin once again in their rematch.

UFC 77 Seemingly falling out of the sky into the Octagon in 2006, Anderson Silva may have been a newcomer to UFC fans, but his international résumé spoke for itself. By the end of that first year though, everyone knew how good "The Spider" was, as he took the UFC middleweight crown from respected champion Rich Franklin via first-round knockout at UFC 64. A year and a half later, in October of 2007, they met again in the main event of UFC 77, and it wasn't one blow from Silva that ended the rematch with Franklin, but a wide array of techniques that looked like they came out of a videogame. The second-round barrage was a thing of beauty, and it left Franklin not only helpless, but with a look on his face wondering what the best pound-for-pound fighter in the world was going to unleash on him next.

"I apologize to Rich for beating him in his home town. I am so sorry."
Anderson Silva

A close fight with Terry Etim becomes a highlight reel knockout for Edson Barboza at UFC 142.

UFC 142 ESPN's ESPY awards certainly got it wrong in not awarding this its 2012 Play of the Year award, but the finalist there is a winner in everyone else's book because in a sport with several spectacular knockouts, Edson Barboza's wheel kick finish of Terry Etim at UFC 142 in January of 2012 was far and away one of the best. It had it all – speed, power, technique, accuracy, and pure 'wow' effect. Etim was out the second he got caught by Barboza, and the scary part is that when asked about the finisher, the Brazilian Muay Thai expert said, "To be honest, no, I don't train that kick much. But I've known how to do that kick since I was eight years old, when I started training Muay Thai. I think I have been keeping it inside of my mind, and when I need it I throw it out."

Matt Hughes KO2 Carlos Newton

UFC 34 A charismatic and dynamic fighter, Carlos Newton was seen by many as someone who could carry the UFC's welterweight division. Veteran Matt Hughes had other ideas, and he used his freakish strength to establish control of their UFC 34 bout in November of 2001 from the outset. With slams, knees, and strikes, Hughes easily won the first round, and was dominating the second, when Newton was able to nab him in a triangle choke. In response, Hughes lifted Newton over his head and drove him into the fence. The champion grabbed the top of the fence, but soon let go after being admonished by referee John McCarthy. With Newton still over his head, and still sinking in the choke, Hughes took a step back and dropped his foe to the mat. Slamming his head on the canvas, Newton was out and a new champion—Matt Hughes—was crowned.

Carlos Newton goes for an armbar on Matt Hughes.

"I heard the ref say the fight's over, but I thought he meant I'd won."
Carlos Newton

Gabriel Gonzaga KO1 Mirko Cro Cop

Gabe Gonzaga celebrates while Mirko CroCop receives attenion.

UFC 70 Many felt that Gabriel Gonzaga's ground game was good enough that if he could take Mirko Cro Cop to the mat, he had a chance to win. Well, Gonzaga followed that plan and grounded and pounded Cro Cop for much of the opening round of their UFC 70 bout in 2007. Unfortunately for the Brazilian, his efforts seemed for naught when the fight was stood up with 35 seconds left in the round. Suddenly, Gonzaga was going to face the wrath of the most feared striker in the game. But then a funny thing happened, and Gonzaga whipped a right kick to Cro Cop's head, and the Croatian fell like he was shot, grotesquely twisting his knee and ankle in the process. Not only was it shocking, it was spectacular, as Cro Cop got defeated by the weapon he had made his reputation with—a kick to the head.w

"I'm not just a BJJ guy – I can knock you out too!"
Gabriel Gonzaga

WEIGHT DIVISIONS

From the days of no weight classes to today's UFC, where nine divisions have found homes in the Octagon, it's been a wild ride.

Brock Lesnar vs. Jose Aldo. Jon Jones vs. Dominick Cruz. Anderson Silva vs. Urijah Faber. If those six fighters had been competing in the early days of the Ultimate Fighting Championship, those are the matchups you might have seen because back then there were no weight classes. So it was routine to see Royce Gracie giving up significant amounts of weight to opponents like Dan Severn, or the most extreme example of all, 600lb Emmanuel Yarborough fighting 200lb Keith Hackney at UFC 3 in 1994.

It was certainly spectacle more than sport, and no one will deny that some of those outrageous bouts were entertaining, but as the UFC began evolving, something needed to be done not just to add clarity, but to protect the fighters from mismatches that could turn ugly.

Finally, at UFC 12 in 1997, the change began, as the organization implemented two weight classes—heavyweight and lightweight. Heavyweights were 200lb and over, and lightweights were 199lb and under. It wasn't the perfect solution, but it was a start, and that night, the UFC's first heavyweight champion—Mark Coleman—was crowned.

At UFC Japan later that year, the 199lb division (now called middleweight) had its first champion, Frank Shamrock, and by March of 1998, the lightweights were reborn as 170lb and below. Pat Miletich was the first titleholder in this new weight class, and one of the fighters he coached, Jens Pulver, competed in the new bantamweight division (for fighters 155lb and below) at UFC 26 in 2000.

By November of 2000, the unified rules of mixed martial arts that are still used today were drawn up and adopted, and five weight classes were implemented by the UFC – heavyweight, light heavyweight, middleweight, welterweight, and lightweight. Everything stayed that way in the Octagon until late 2010, when it was announced that the UFC was bringing in the featherweight (145lb) and bantamweight (135lb) divisions into the organization, and in 2012, the flyweights (125lb) entered the Octagon, with a 135-pound women's bantamweight class implemented in 2013.

Mark Hominick grounds and pounds Jose Aldo in the fight of the night at UFC 129.

FLYWEIGHT FIGHTERS

At 125 pounds, the flyweights are the smallest fighters competing in the UFC, but these all-action athletes definitely pack a punch.

John Dodson

A top five flyweight with speed, power, and athleticism, John Dodson won his first three UFC fights, defeating TJ Dillashaw, Tim Elliott, and Jussier Formiga before losing a close decision to flyweight champion Demetrious Johnson in January of 2013.

John Moraga

To call John Moraga's rise in the UFC meteoric would be understating the matter, as the former Arizona State University wrestler stormed onto the scene with finishes of Ulysses Gomez and Chris Cariaso in 2012, earning him a shot at the flyweight title in July of 2013.

Joseph Benavidez

A longtime bantamweight contender in both the WEC and UFC, Joseph Benavidez was finally given a level playing field to compete on with the creation of the flyweight division in the UFC. In 2012, Benavidez debuted at 125 pounds in style in 2012, knocking out Yasuhiro Urushitani before engaging in a classic championship bout with Demetrious Johnson in September of that year.

John Lineker

Brazilian banger John Lineker is one of the most entertaining fighters in the flyweight division today, and with his ability to end a bout with one punch, he has most certainly earned his nickname "Hands of Stone."

Demetrious Johnson

It's been said in the fight game that it's harder to defend a title than win it, but Demetrious "Mighty Mouse" Johnson, the first flyweight champion in UFC history, appears to be doing just fine so far, as he successfully retained his 125-pound crown twice already.

BANTAMWEIGHT FIGHTERS

Despite being one of the smallest weight class in the UFC, the 135lb bantamweights deliver heavyweight action when the bell rings.

Renan Barao

When Dominick Cruz was sidelined by a knee injury, Brazil's Renan Barao more than ably stepped into the champion's shoes as the interim UFC titleholder at 135 pounds. In 2013, Barao made the first defense of his title, forcing Michael McDonald to tap out in the fourth round.

Urijah Faber

After nearly three years atop the featherweight division, former WEC champion Urijah Faber's name was synonymous with excellence at 145lb. But some believe that he may be even better 10lb south at bantamweight, and his wins over Takeya Mizugaki and Eddie Wineland thus far have proved it.

Brad Pickett

One of England's top fighters, Brad Pickett took his game to the United States and the WEC in 2009, debuting with a win over Kyle Dietz and introducing fans to his all-action style. The next step saw him attempt to make his mark in the UFC, and after four post fight bonus-winning efforts, he's done just that.

Eddie Wineland

In 2006, Eddie Wineland became the first man to hold the WEC bantamweight title. In 2010, he was tearing up the organization again, running off three consecutive wins before earning a berth in the UFC, where he debuted in 2011 with a co-main event bout at UFC 128 against Urijah Faber.

Dominick Cruz

One of the most difficult puzzles to figure out in MMA is that of Dominick Cruz, whose unorthodox style and pinpoint-accurate striking has led him to wins in 17 of 18 fights as well as the UFC bantamweight title, which he hopes to defend successfully in 2011 and beyond.

FEATHERWEIGHT FIGHTERS

Once the WEC's flagship division, the featherweights have turned into one of the most exciting weight classes in the UFC.

Chad Mendes

Former WEC featherweight champ Urijah Faber always said that Chad Mendes would make an immediate impression once he hit the big show, and "Money" has done just that, winning five consecutive WEC / UFC bouts against the likes of Michihiro Omigawa, Erik Koch, Anthony Morrison, Cub Swanson, and Javier Vazquez.

Jose Aldo

Whether it's his lightning-fast kicks and knees, or laser-like punches, the attack of Brazilian powerhouse Jose Aldo has taken him to the top of the featherweight division, and he's barely been challenged, with Urijah Faber and Mike Brown among the top-shelf fighters unable to figure him out.

Chan Sung Jung

Better known to fight fans as "The Korean Zombie," Chan Sung Jung's slugging style has been augmented by a deadly ground game in recent years, and after picking up post-fight bonuses in three straight wins over Leonard Garcia, Mark Hominick, and Dustin Poirier, you have to wonder what he can possibly do for an encore.

Frankie Edgar

As 2010 dawned, people knew that Frankie Edgar was good, but it wasn't until his upset win over BJ Penn for the UFC lightweight title in April that they knew just how good "The Answer" could be. And with two defenses under his belt, he may be on top for a long time.

Cub Swanson

Perennial featherweight contender Cub Swanson may have a Brazilian Jiu-Jitsu black belt, but it's his striking that led him to Knockout of the Night wins over Ross Pearson and Charles Oliveira and subsequent victories against Dustin Poirier and Dennis Siver.

LIGHTWEIGHT FIGHTERS

Throughout UFC history, few divisions have had a ride like the lightweights. Here are five fighters that made it a memorable one.

Jens Pulver

One of the lighter weight classes' most respected pioneers, Jens Pulver's legacy in the sport of MMA is secure. And with his memorable wins over BJ Penn, Caol Uno, and Cub Swanson, the first UFC lightweight champion, known as "Lil' Evil," has set a standard that is truly inspiring.

Anthony Pettis

Former WEC lightweight champion Anthony Pettis took a little while to get acclimated to the UFC in 2011, splitting two fights with Clay Guida and Jeremy Stephens. But by 2012, "Showtime" was back, with highlight reel finishes of Joe Lauzon and Donald "Cowboy" Cerrone earning the Milwaukee native two Knockout of the Night bonuses.

Gilbert Melendez

After a record-shattering stint in Strikeforce that saw him set records for most wins and most successful title defenses, it was more than time for Gilbert Melendez to make his move to the Octagon, and after a close five round battle with UFC lightweight boss Benson Henderson in April of 2013, it was evident that the reputation of "El Nino" as one of the best in the world was well-deserved.

Kenny Florian

With nine wins at 155 pounds, The Ultimate Fighter season one's Kenny Florian earned his place among the top lightweights in the world, defeating some of the best in the game along the way, including Takanori Gomi and Joe Lauzon. And though he fell short of winning a world title at lightweight and featherweight, the retired "Ken Flo" left the game with a legacy to be proud of.

Benson Henderson

Benson Henderson's reign over the lightweight division began in 2012 with his wins over Frankie Edgar (twice) and Nate Diaz, and "Smooth" tightened his grip on the crown in April of 2013 when he pounded out a five round split decision win over former Strikeforce champion Gilbert Melendez.

WELTERWEIGHT FIGHTERS

Home to some of the most talented fighters in the UFC, the welterweights have been primarily ruled by two men —Matt Hughes and Georges St-Pierre.

Georges St-Pierre

One of the most dominant champions ever, welterweight titleholder Georges St-Pierre has defeated the best the division has to offer, and with wins over BJ Penn, Matt Hughes, Thiago Alves, and Jon Fitch, the pride of Montreal, Quebec, has set the standard for mixed martial arts fighters from Canada.

Matt Hughes

Perhaps the greatest champion in UFC history, Matt Hughes defended his welterweight crown seven times over two reigns, defeating Georges St-Pierre, BJ Penn, and Sean Sherk in the process. In May of 2010, Hughes was inducted into the UFC Hall of Fame for his Octagon achievements, an honor well deserved.

Royce Gracie

If you think fighting once a night is tough, consider that Royce Gracie— the man who introduced the world to jiu-jitsu and MMA in 1993—did it three times in one night to win the UFC 1 tournament, four times at UFC 2, and three times at UFC 3.

Johny Hendricks

A four-time All-American for Oklahoma State University, Johny Hendricks is already one of the most accomplished wrestlers competing in the UFC today. Yet surprisingly, his MMA reputation was cemented with his hands, most notably first round knockouts of Martin Kampmann and Jon Fitch.

BJ Penn

As one of two men in UFC history to win titles in two weight classes, former welterweight and lightweight champion BJ Penn has lived up to his nickname, "The Prodigy," but the pride of Hilo, Hawaii, still has goals to reach in the Octagon, and doubters would be foolish to count him out.

MIDDLEWEIGHT FIGHTERS

Big enough to hit plenty hard but small enough for serious speed, the 185lb division boasts its share of Octagon icons.

Anderson Silva

"The Spider" is, quite simply, the greatest. It is hard to imagine anyone breaking the dozens of records the Brazilian has set. The stats alone tell the story: longest UFC winning streak (16) and longest title reign (seven years). But throw in a list of those he has defeated, elite fighters including Rich Franklin, Dan Henderson, Chael Sonnen and Vitor Belfort, and you have the UFC's answer to Pele.

Chael Sonnen

An All-American wrestler with a ninth-degree black belt in smack talk, the provocative Sonnen is certainly going to be remembered long after he's retired. His wins against elite contenders Nate Marquardt, Brian Stann and Michael Bisping prove "The American Gangster" is more than a mouth.

Michael Bisping

"The Count" is the most polarizing fighter in UFC history. But love or loathe the Brash Brit, you can't deny his success at 185 pounds, which includes dominant wins against Chris Leben, Brian Stann and Alan Belcher, as well as Fight of the Night victories against Denis Kang and Yoshihiro Akiyama.

Chris Weidman

If the average fan didn't give the previously unbeaten NCAA Division I wrestler a chance against Anderson Silva when they clashed at UFC 162, his peers certainly did. Fighters like Georges St-Pierre, Sonnen, Bisping and Dominick Cruz all said they believed the Age of the Spider would end at the fists of New Yorker Weidman. They were right.

Rich Franklin

One of only two men to defend the middleweight belt more than once, "Ace" scalped Evan Tanner, David Loiseau, and Yushin Okami at 185lb. Although he lost to Anderson Silva twice, his second career at 205lb—which yielded wins over both Wanderlei Silva and Chuck Liddell—cemented the Ohio man's legacy.

LIGHT HEAVYWEIGHT

Some of the biggest stars in history, including Chuck Liddell and Jon Jones, have established 205lb as the sport's flagship division.

Chuck Liddell

Perhaps more than any other, "The Iceman" embodied the UFC: exciting, uncompromising, and, well, just cool. The former accounting major from California is also the greatest striker to ever throw down in the Octagon, with Randy Couture, Tito Ortiz, and Wanderlei Silva all falling to the Hall of Famer.

Forrest Griffin

The original "Ultimate Fighter," the former Georgia cop turned 205lb champ has parlayed his quirky sense of humor from reality TV stardom to TV host and bestselling author. But his in-Octagon achievements are impressive too, as wins over Tito Ortiz, Rampage Jackson, and Shogun Rua earned him a well-deserved Hall of Fame spot upon his July 2013 retirement.

Jon Jones

"Bones" has been on a reign of terror at 205 pounds, ever since becoming the youngest-ever UFC world champion in March 2011 at age 23. He is an outstanding wrestler who uses his pterodactyl-like 84.5-inch reach to spear opponents with easily the most innovative striking arsenal in the UFC. Jones is something truly special and, terrifyingly, is only getting better.

Rashad Evans

"Suga" fought his way to the The Ultimate Fighter season two tournament title, despite being inexperienced and fighting much bigger men as a heavyweight. He immediately dropped down to 205 pounds and became one of the division's great talents, beating talent including Chuck Liddell, Tito Oritz, Rampage Jackson and Forrest Griffin.

Tito Ortiz

He may have scored only one win in his last nine fights as a UFC fighter, but we should remember in his 1999-2004 prime, Ortiz was a fearsome champion. His victories against Wanderlei Silva, Vitor Belfort and Forrest Griffin, plus three wins in a highly toxic feud with Ken Shamrock, earned the "Huntington Beach Bad Boy" his Hall of Fame spot.

The raw power of Brock Lesnar or uncanny speed of Cain Velasquez have led even Mike Tyson to acknowledge the holder of the UFC heavyweight belt is the "baddest man on the planet."

Cain Velasquez

The first Mexican-American heavyweight champion in any combat sport, soft-spoken Cain couldn't even find fights, such was his reputation in the gym, so he joined the UFC after two bouts. He is twice the UFC champion, with only nemesis Junior Dos Santos seemingly able to give him a fight.

Frank Mir

One of the first big men to use BJJ as his primary weapon, Mir shot to fame as a precociously talented 20-something in the early 2000s. However, he had to overcome a career-threatening motorcycle accident, as well as Lesnar and Minotauro Nogueira, to regain the title he never lost in the Octagon.

Junior "Cerano" Dos Santos

Once so poor he could barely afford to eat, the Brazilian powerhouse known as "JDS" blasted his way from the South American slums all the way to the top of the UFC. Easily the hardest puncher to ever step in the Octagon, he has already held the world title, and many predict another reign.

Mark Coleman

The first of the powerful wrestlers to adapt his collegiate skills to the Octagon, Hall of Famer "The Hammer" will forever be known as "The Godfather of Ground and Pound." It was Coleman who popularized the technique of using wrestling to take down and trap opponents before smashing them with strikes.

Brock Lesnar

The former NCAA champion and pro wrestling star astonished everyone by smashing Randy Couture to annex the UFC title after just three pro fights at UFC 91. Second-round wins against both Frank Mir and Shane Carwin followed, but a life-threatening stomach condition forced Lesnar to retire in 2011 with a unique 5-3 legacy.

34

WOMEN'S BANTAMWEIGHT *FIGHTERS*

In February of 2013, the ladies of mixed martial arts made their way to the Octagon, and fans have been treated to epic and exciting ever since.

Miesha Tate

A former Strikeforce bantamweight champion, Miesha Tate is a female fighting pioneer, having competed in the sport since 2007. But she is not looking to rest on her laurels, and following fights with Julie Kedzie and Cat Zingano, she will get a rematch with champion Ronda Rousey.

Sara McMann

One of the most decorated athletes to ever step foot in the Octagon, 2004 Olympic Silver medal winner Sara McMann has proven herself on the international stage as a freestyle wrestler, and now she's looking forward to doing the same thing in the UFC.

Cat Zingano

An accomplished high school and college wrestler, Cat Zingano parlayed her skill on the mats into a new passion when she discovered Brazilian Jiu-Jitsu and MMA. In April of 2013, she made her UFC debut against Miesha Tate a successful one, winning in the third round.

Sarah Kaufman

Sarah Kaufman grew from an unknown prizefighter from Victoria, British Columbia, Canada to one of the top 135-pound fighters in the world, earning a Strikeforce bantamweight title in the process while defeating Miesha Tate, Liz Carmouche, and Roxanne Modafferi.

Ronda Rousey

In 2013, Ronda Rousey, the first ever UFC women's champion, made history when she successfully defended her bantamweight crown with a first round armbar submission over Liz Carmouche, leading the former Olympic Bronze medalist in judo to a coaching stint on The Ultimate Fighter.

ARIANNY CELESTE

The most popular young lady in the UFC organization, the lovely Arianny Celeste has the ability to send countless hearts racing in the time it takes her to walk around the perimeter of the Octagon.

Arianny Celeste became a UFC Octagon Girl in typical fashion—through a modeling casting call—but ever since she made her debut in 2006, life has been anything but typical for the Las Vegas native, who saw her first live mixed martial arts fight that night. And the way she sees it, the sky's the limit on just how far this sport can go.

"It's definitely being recognized as a sport more than just two guys going at it," said the striking Latina. "People are aware of the skill involved behind what the fighters are doing. We're traveling around the world now, it's huge and it's just getting bigger."

And as the UFC has grown, so has Arianny's notoriety, not only as a popular model who has appeared on the covers of *Playboy* and *Maxim* magazines, but also in the music world, where she is a talented singer currently recording her first CD.

But as far as she's concerned, nothing beats being Octagonside in the best seat in the house for a UFC event.

"It's very exciting and it's like an adrenaline rush, especially when it's a big pay-per-view fight," she said. "It's a lot of fun."

The lovely Arianny Celeste does her stuff at the UFC Fight for the Troops event.

QUOTES

Some UFC fighters let their fists and feet do the talking. But most are as adept in front of a microphone as they are when the bell rings. Check out these quotes to see why.

"Being great is one thing, but being remembered is another thing. To be great, magnificent, and remembered, you have to stand for something and change the world in a way. I want to change the world."
Jon Jones

"No nerves. At that moment there's nowhere to run. If you trained, you trained; if you didn't, you're screwed."
Anderson Silva

"I'm trying to spread the word of MMA and what it's really about. It's not some thugs getting into a cage and trying to kill each other. We're trained athletes, educated, smart, and we understand the business side of it—at least some of us do. I've understood that from day one, and I think that's why the fanbase that I have is as big as it is—it's because I understood the extra stuff and I want to not only be an inspiration, but a role model to a lot of kids so I can let them know that through hard work and dedication, they can achieve anything."
Tito Ortiz

"At the end of the day, this is the fight business. We aren't fight friends. This isn't Eminem insulting 50 Cent during an interview from across the country. If somebody's got a problem with what I've said, well, let's go fight. We can settle this. We don't have to do this through the media and sing songs about it, we can also just go fight. So anytime this gets me in trouble, the solution to the problem is very evident – it's an eight-sided cage called the Octagon – I'll see you there."
Chael Sonnen

"You only live once. In my mind, I think I'm a good enough athlete that I could do just about anything, and I always had a lot of confidence. But young kids today need to remember that—that when you work hard and stay on track, good things usually come. It doesn't happen overnight, but if you keep your nose to the grindstone, hopefully good things happen."
Brock Lesnar

"I think the challenge for every fighter is to pick yourself up, evaluate, dust yourself off, and get back in there. Learn from your mistakes, make adjustments, and go out and compete again. That's the mark of that championship spirit. I've certainly been in that position before and I find myself there again, so I look forward to the opportunity to go back out there and get after it."
Randy Couture

"I never got in this to be famous, make money, or necessarily to put fights on for the fans, and as weird as this sounds, it's about me and my growth as a fighter and trying to get better. And once that dies, it's time for me to hang up the gloves."
Kenny Florian

TOP 10 UFC®

SUBMISSIONS OF ALL TIME

To the true UFC connoisseur, there's nothing better than a well-executed submission, as it can be the exclamation point on a dominating performance, or the move that rescues victory from the jaws of defeat.

Anderson Silva Wsub5 Chael Sonnen

UFC 117 No, it didn't have the technical wizardry of some of the Octagon's most amazing tap-out finishes, and yes, eight of number-one middleweight contender Chael Sonnen's 11 pro losses have come via submission, but on the sport's most pressure-filled stage, and with his championship reign slipping away, 185lb champion Anderson "The Spider" Silva pulled off a submission for the ages as he sunk in a triangle-armbar on Sonnen that finished the UFC 117 main event at 3:10 of the fifth round. That was impressive enough. Doing it after taking nearly five rounds of punishment from a determined challenger while sporting a pre-fight rib injury lifts Silva's feat to another level. It was good watching it on tape after the fact, no question about it; but live at the Oracle Arena that night in August of 2010, the atmosphere was electric, and few who were there will ever forget it.

Anderson Silva spent nearly five rounds on his back, getting punched by Chael Sonnen, making his UFC 117 win even more amazing.

Matt Hughes Wsub1 Frank Trigg

Matt Hughes was able to escape this punishing choking move from Frank Trigg.

UFC 52 The UFC 52 bout between Matt Hughes and Frank Trigg in April of 2005 packed more drama into 4:05 than most do in five rounds, definitively putting it on the list of best UFC fights of all time. After an intense opening staredown, Trigg caught Hughes with a low knee in the early going that was not caught by referee Mario Yamasaki. As Hughes tried to regain his bearings, Trigg pounced and sent him to the canvas with a left to the jaw. In serious trouble, Hughes wound up giving Trigg his back for a rear naked choke. Hughes' face turned crimson, but amazingly he was able to escape and follow up by picking his foe up and carrying him across the cage before dropping him on his back. Now it was Hughes in control, and he sunk in his own rear naked choke, which produced a tap out at the 4:05 mark.

"That's what a champion does. He keeps fighting!"
Matt Hughes

BJ Penn Wsub1 Matt Hughes

UFC 46 BJ Penn was in an interesting place in his life after he was upset in his first world title bout by Jens Pulver in 2002. Returning four months later, "The Prodigy" stopped Paul Creighton in two less than compelling rounds and he then won a close decision over Matt Serra in a bout some believed the New Yorker won, before fighting Caol Uno for the title Pulver vacated. An unsatisfying five-round draw followed. A win over Takanori Gomi in a non-UFC bout in Hawaii was a more positive result, but it wasn't until his return at UFC 46 in January of 2004 that people got a glimpse of the "real" BJ Penn again, as he moved up 15lb to the welterweight division and shocked the world with a first-round submission of the seemingly unbeatable Matt Hughes. At long last, BJ Penn was a champion.

BJ Penn moved up to welterweight division and beat Matt Hughes with a first-round submission.

Frank Mir Wsub1 Tim Sylvia

 Unbeaten in his first four mixed martial arts bouts, including two in the UFC, Frank Mir was expected to be the heavyweight division's Golden Boy as soon as he got a shot at the title. But an upset loss to Ian Freeman in 2002 derailed Mir's road to the title, and it wasn't until he scored a win over Tank Abbott and two more victories over Wes Sims that he was able to earn a shot at the vacant UFC heavyweight title against Tim Sylvia at UFC 48 in June of 2004. Of course, Mir's image had taken a hit with the loss to Freeman, but a win over Sylvia would erase those memories, and that's what Mir did, taking only 50 seconds to lock Sylvia's arm up and break it, forcing a stoppage to the bout. Finally, Frank Mir was now UFC heavyweight champion.

Frank Mir pops Tim Sylvia's forearm at UFC 48.

Royce Gracie Wsub1 Ken Shamrock

UFC 1 Poor Royce Gracie. Sure, the skinny kid from Brazil was impressive in submitting pro boxer Art Jimmerson in his first UFC bout on November 12, 1993, but his next opponent in the tournament that night was the physically imposing Ken Shamrock, someone who not only held the physical edge on Gracie, but also knew a thing or two about submission fighting. But once in the Octagon, it was Gracie who prevailed in this battle of future Hall of Famers, forcing Shamrock to tap out to a rear naked choke just 57 seconds into the bout. It was the second of three wins Gracie scored in Denver, earning himself the first UFC tournament victory and beginning what was a legendary career. As for his rivalry with Shamrock, the two would meet again, at UFC 5 in 1995, fighting to a 36-minute draw.

Chan Sung Jung Wsub2 Leonard Garcia

UFC FIGHT NIGHT 24

Before Chan Sung Jung's March 2011 rematch with Leonard Garcia, you might have assumed that the fight game of "The Korean Zombie" started and finished with his ability to brawl. Maybe "Bad Boy" Garcia, who defeated Jung in their classic 2010 bout, figured the same thing. He might have even thought that he was safe as the seconds wound down in round two of their bout in Louisville, Kentucky. But that's when Jung struck with Eddie Bravo's "Twister," a painful maneuver that had never finished a fight in the UFC – well, up until Garcia's tap out at 4:59 of the second round. It was a beautifully executed move, and a historic one that has yet to be replicated in the Octagon.

Chan Sung Jang turned the tables on Leonard Garcia with this historic Twister submission.

Dustin Hazelett completes the armbar on Josh Burkman.

Dustin Hazelett Wsub2 Josh Burkman

TUF 7 UFC color commentator Joe Rogan described Dustin Hazelett's submission victory over Josh Burkman at *The Ultimate Fighter 7 Finale* in June of 2008 as "probably the sweetest armbar I have ever seen in mixed martial arts." And it's hard to argue with him. But when you ask the humble jiu-jitsu wizard about the move that earned tons of Submission of the Year accolades, he admits that it was a happy accident. "Most of the moves I practice and plan, except for the armbar on Burkman, which I kinda just made up on the spot. And when I did it, I had no clue how I ended up in the armbar. (Laughs) I was just trying to take him down, and the next thing I knew, I was in an armbar. It looked like I meant to do it and that I practiced it, but I've never done it before or since."

*"A great submission— like a great KO
— just comes out of nowhere."*
Joe Rogan

Murilo Bustamante Wsub1 Matt Lindland

UFC 37 It's hard enough to pull off a submission on a world-class opponent vying for his first UFC title. To do it twice in the same fight is beyond comprehension. But that's just what Murilo Bustamante did in the first defense of his UFC middleweight championship against Matt Lindland at UFC 37 in May of 2002. Late in the opening round, Bustamante caught Lindland with an armbar and "The Law" apparently tapped. Yet after referee John McCarthy halted the action, Lindland claimed that he didn't surrender and the bout was restarted. Bustamante, upset but resilient, went back to work, and in the third round he sunk in a guillotine choke. This time, Lindland's tap stood, and the Brazilian Jiu-Jitsu ace had retained his title in what was not only one of the most bizarre bouts in UFC history, but one of the best displays of black-belt-level grappling as well.

Bustamante managed to pull off two submissions against Lindland.

Karo Parisyan Wsub1 Dave Strasser

UFC 44 Shocking those observers who didn't believe judo had a place in mixed martial arts, UFC newcomer Karo Parisyan put on a judo clinic against veteran Dave Strasser at UFC 44 in September of 2003, submitting his foe impressively with a rarely seen rolling kimura at 3:52 of the first round after a series of impressive maneuvers that dazzled the Las Vegas crowd. It was a moment that will stay with "The Heat" forever. "It's something that you never forget," said Parisyan, a longtime welterweight contender. "The first fight when I came in, it went very well and I think it was my most technical and dominating performance that I ever had in the UFC. I remember being a kid coming in—I was just 21 years old—trying to push the fight, and there was a lot of hype about me in the beginning."

Karo Parisyan overcame Dave Strasser with a rarely seen rolling kimura at UFC 44.

Matt Hughes Wsub1 Georges St-Pierre

Matt Hughes becomes the first man to beat— and sub—"GSP."

UFC 50 Matt Hughes' return to the Octagon less than five months after he lost his welterweight title in a stunning upset to BJ Penn was an uneventful but victorious one, as he decisioned Renato Verissimo. That propelled him into a bout for the vacant crown against unbeaten Canadian young gun Georges St-Pierre. St-Pierre had already made a lot of noise in the UFC, but Hughes was not about to let another chance for the top spot slip away. It made for an intriguing matchup on paper, and despite only lasting one round, the UFC 50 fight on October 22, 2004 delivered on its promise. After a slow start, Hughes bounced back and began pounding away on his foe from the guard. But practically everyone in the arena was surprised when Hughes beautifully transitioned into an armbar to end the match with a single second left in the first round.

"He's going to be a great fighter one day, but I am the champ tonight."
Matt Hughes on Georges St-Pierre

UFC AROUND THE WORLD

The incredible rise of the Ultimate Fighting Championship over the last two decades has seen athletes from literally all over the world step forward to test themselves in the ultimate proving ground, the UFC Octagon.

Georges St-Pierre hears the roar of the record 55,724 crowd at the Rogers Centre, Toronto, at UFC 129.

In less than 20 years, the UFC has grown from a supposed one-off spectacle to the fastest growing sports organization in history with UFC programming available on TV all over the world.

With literally tens and tens of millions of fans watching UFC events each and every month—from the US to Canada, from the UK to Italy and the Middle East to Japan and New Zealand—it is no surprise that the current UFC roster features fighters from every corner of the globe.

The original eight men who competed in UFC 1 in 1993 represented three nationalities: Brazilian, American, and the Dutch. Fast forward to the present day and it is not uncommon to find seven countries represented on a card.

Dana White believes this process will only accelerate during his second decade as UFC President: "Mixed martial arts is blowing up all over the world, MMA gyms are springing up, and kids who are growing up watching the UFC are learning mixed martial arts. Listen, America is never going to get cricket, and in Europe they are never going to care about basketball or baseball—they just don't get it.

"But I can take two fighters, put them in an Octagon and you win by KO, submission, or on points, and everyone gets it. You don't even need to hear the commentary, you get it. Fighting is in our DNA, always has been and always will be, Nothing brings people together like a great fight, and the UFC puts on the best fights between the greatest fighters on the planet."

For White, the allure of the Octagon is simple. He said: "You can be the fastest runner on the field, or shoot the best hoop or kick this ball through this goal better than everyone else but, at the end of the day, what truly matters is being the toughest guy in the world. In the UFC, these guys prove they are the ultimate athletes, the toughest of the tough. But it is not for everyone. Most people can't do what these guys do, that's why watching them is so cool."

At the time of publication, more than 200 UFC events have taken place in more than 50 cities in the U.S.; 14 have taken place in the UK and Canada, nine in Brazil, six in Japan, five in Australia, two in Germany, China and Sweden and one a piece in Puerto Rico and the United Arab Emirates.

While the UFC and matchmakers Joe Silva and Sean Shelby often try to have "local" fighters represented on the card, one of the unique aspects of the UFC as a live sporting spectacle is that crowds are uncharacteristically unpartisan.

White said: "If you are a UFC fan, most of the time you are going to cheer for your favorite because you like his fighting style or like his personality, not just because he's from the same country as you. For years Georges St-Pierre has been cheered in America more loudly than his opponent, and he's been fighting Americans in America.

"You have Brazilians who barely speak English in the UFC, who are loved by the fans in America, in England, and all over the world."

"We have just nine world championships, one per division. It's got more to do with how you fight in the Octagon than what it says on your passport."

The multinationalism of the sport is reflected in the value of the UFC World Championships, White said. "We looked at what boxing has been doing wrong and did the opposite. We have just nine world champions, one per division. If you are the UFC Champion you are the best in the world and you defend that title against the best in the world three or four times a year. There's none of this idea where a champion gets to pick opponents and defend in his hometown every time. If you are the UFC champion, that means you fight the best guys no matter where they are from and no matter where the fight is."

UFC IN THE US

Boasting more than 30 UFC champions and nine Hall of Fame fighters, the US is the UFC superpower.

Just as the UFC has helped showcase Brazilian Jiu-Jitsu as a legitimately effective martial art, so too has the predominantly American combat sport of wrestling had its mettle proved in the furnace heat of the UFC Octagon.

The combat sport which would eventually become known as freestyle or collegiate wrestling was developed in the US and UK in the early 19th century but, while interest waned in Britain, wrestling became almost a way of life across the US, with no fewer than six US presidents competing at some point in their lives and college programs exploding across the country.

With the advent of the UFC, collegiate wrestlers were given a chance to continue legitimate competition after graduation. Dan Severn, Randy Couture, and Mark Coleman were among the first of the American wrestlers to storm the UFC, combating the previous advantages of submission grapplers with their use of strategic takedowns and top control.

The National Anthem at UFC Fight for the Troops 2, January 22, 2011 in Fort Hood.

As the years rolled on and the sport developed, American wrestlers like Matt Hughes, Rashad Evans, Jon Fitch, Josh Koscheck, Chuck Liddell, Dan Henderson and Chris Weidman continued to pile proof upon the undeniable fact that wrestling is the perfect starting base on which to build a complete martial artist.

In fact, five of the 10 fighters in the UFC Hall of Fame—Dan Severn, Randy Couture, Mark Coleman, Chuck Liddell, and Matt Hughes—were National Collegiate Athletic Association Division I wrestlers before they competed in MMA.

Hughes explained the importance of both: "In MMA, you have to be the one making the choice as to whether the fight stays standing or goes to the ground. Strong wrestling enables you to make that choice. If you want to keep standing, like Chuck Liddell usually did, wrestling allows you to stuff takedowns or get up if you are taken down. It teaches you to scramble. And if you want the fight on the ground, a good single- or double-leg beats any other type of takedown in my view."

While Zuffa's view of the UFC has always been that its a global sport, undoubtedly the USA will forever remain the cornerstone of the company. Dana White said: "Fighting is in our DNA. We get it, and we like it. I don't care if you are from New York, Las Vegas, Hawaii, or Texas, Americans like combat sports."

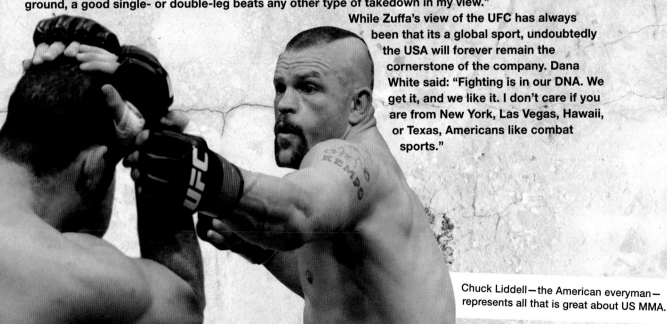

Chuck Liddell—the American everyman— represents all that is great about US MMA.

UFC® IN CANADA

Perhaps Canada would not be the first country you would think of if someone mentioned Ultimate Fighting, but it probably should be.

While the US, the UK, and the spiritual home of modern martial arts—Brazil—were "no-brainers" for the UFC to attain crossover success, Canada most certainly was not. While the Canuck sports fan is well known to ice hockey enthusiasts, with little real heritage of combat sports north of the US border, the idea that Canada would become "the Mecca of MMA" would have seem far-fetched a decade ago.

The face of Canadian martial arts—Georges St-Pierre.

"We never saw Canada coming," admitted Dana White. "This thing has just blown up in that country. I'd have a show up there every day if I could."

Canada had been producing quality fighters for years; so many, in fact, that the UFC decided to promote 2006's UFC 58 as "USA vs. Canada." However, it took a little while for the legislation to be put into place for the UFC to debut in the Great White North, but that only built anticipation to a fever pitch among Canadian fans. When it was confirmed that UFC 83 would emanate from the Bell Centre in Montreal on April 19, 2008, and that local hero Georges St-Pierre would get his chance to avenge his world title defeat to Matt Serra in the main event, tickets exploded out of the box office.

UFC 83 set two company records: the fastest sell-out (1 minute of public sale with all other seats going to UFC Fight Club members) and the largest attendance ever at 21,390 for a UFC event. Although the fastest sell-out record was equaled by UFC 127 in Sydney, Australia, the records set by Canada's second largest city remained in place for over three years… until the UFC made its debut in Canada's largest city.

UFC 129 shattered records left and right and raised the bar for what is now expected from a sporting supershow. The cavernous Rogers Centre sold out its 55,724 tickets immediately and the 60ft wrap-around high-res superscreen was unlike anything sports fans had been treated to previously.

In the main event, Canadian national institution St-Pierre—who is so beloved in Canada he has been voted "Athlete of the Year" for three years running by the prestigious Rogers Sportsnet—defeated Jake Shields despite fighting for most of the five rounds with one eye injured.

White said simply: "This was the biggest night in company history. I love Canada."

The UFC has an incredible following in Canada and featherweight Mark Hominick is one of its star fighters.

UFC IN BRAZIL

If Asia is the spiritual home of traditional martial arts, the soul of modern MMA is to be found in Brazil.

While the concept of fusing the most effective aspects of striking and grappling together had already occurred to the ancient Greeks, it is hard to imagine the Ultimate Fighting Championship ever existing without the enormous contributions of Brazil and Brazilian Jiu-Jitsu (BJJ).

The Brazilian Gracie family invented what the world knows today as BJJ and, in fact, played an equally significant role in the creation of the UFC. With his shy smile and slender body, Royce Gracie completely changed the perception that an elite fighter had to be built like a heavily muscled Hollywood action hero when he dominated boxers, wrestlers, and martial artists to win the UFC 1, 2, and 4 tournaments.

But, as significant as the Gracie family contribution is to MMA and the UFC, Brazilian influence on the UFC hardly ends there.

There have been seven Brazilian UFC champions—nine including Minotauro Nogueira's and Renan Barao's interim title reigns—and Curitiba-born Anderson Silva is almost universally recognized as the greatest fighter ever. And the Brazilian birthed gyms—Chute Boxe, Brazilian Top Team, the Black House and the others—have steadily produced a who's who of the world's greatest fighters over the last decade.

The first actual UFC event to originate from Brazil was named simply "UFC Brazil" and took place on October 16, 1998, at Ginasio da Portuguesa.

Pat Miletich defeated Mikey Burnett by split decision to win what would—eventually—become the UFC welterweight championship, and future Brazilian icons Pedro Rizzo and Wanderlei Silva debuted before UFC 185lb champion Frank Shamrock scored a sweet revenge win over John Lober.

It would be many years before the UFC returned to the cradle of MMA. But, in December 2010, the announcement was made that the world's premier MMA event would return to its spiritual home in August of 2011 for UFC 134.

Since then, the Brazilian fans have engendered a reputation as the most passionate UFC followers in the world.

"Those guys are so loud down there," UFC President Dana White said. "It took us a while to get things lined up in Brazil, but we are putting on regular shows there in front of sold-out arenas. When the UFC is on TV, more people watch it than they watch the Brazilian national soccer team. We are on fire in Brazil."

Ever the sportsman, Royce Gracie congratulates conqueror Matt Hughes.

National icon Vitor Belfort—the first of the Brazilian superstrikers.

UFC IN THE UK

The British have long been a boxing powerhouse and so it's not surprising they are an emerging force in UFC.

"When we first bought this company, we knew for sure one of the places that would get this sport right away was the UK," said UFC President Dana White. "They love boxing and tough sports like rugby over there so the UK was a no-brainer."

The UFC's first incursion to Great Britain came in the summer of 2002, when the Octagon sat proudly in the splendor of London's Royal Albert Hall for UFC 38. Despite a hysterical media reception, the fans who snapped up the 3,800 tickets witnessed MMA history.

Matt Hughes went from champion to icon by repeating his welterweight title win over Carlos Newton in the main event, and local fans were thrilled by an emotional win by Englishman Ian Freeman over heavyweight hotshot Frank Mir. There were also hints of the glamorous future of the sport, with supermodel Elle Macpherson among a handful of Octagonside celebrities.

It would take until April 2007 for the company to return to Britain, but the UFC came back in force, opening a full-time office in London and staging 14 events in the UK over the next five years.

Dan Hardy brought British brashness to the UFC.

Without question, the emergence of the talented and charismatic Michael Bisping was a boon for the UFC. After winning TUF 3, Bisping became the first Englander to headline a UFC vs. Rashad Evans in Newark, USA, at UFC 78. He then headlined at home, beating Chris Leben at Birmingham's UFC 89, before leading a team of Brits to a crushing victory over Dan Henderson's Team USA in TUF 9. In 2013 another Manchester fighter Rosi Sexton became the first Briton to compete in the UFC's female division.

In March 2010, Dan "The Outlaw" Hardy became the first Briton to challenge for a world title, showing enormous heart in losing to welterweight king Georges St-Pierre. With MMA gyms opening all over the UK, Bisping believes it is just a matter of time before a Brit lifts UFC gold.

The Count said: "I think British fighters are always going to have to work hard at wrestling because we just don't have that sport in the UK to a top level. But I think I've shown that, with years of hard work, you can develop your grappling. I think one thing you can say about the UK is some of the best fans in the world are here and, hopefully, there will be a British world champion soon.

"And, selfishly, I hope that's me!"

John Hathaway made a joke of 3-1 odds by dominating Diego Sanchez.

UFC IN GERMANY

As the UFC stepped up its international profile, Germany became the first mainland European country to host an event.

On June 13, 2009, Germany became the first mainland European nation to host an Ultimate Fighting Championship event when UFC 99: The Comeback landed at the superb Lanxess Arena in Cologne, Germany.

Headlined by a "catchweight" bout at 195lb between former UFC middleweight champion Rich "Ace" Franklin and former PRIDE middleweight king Wanderlei Silva, the event was greeted with rapture and long-time German UFC fans snapped up 12,854 tickets and roared their approval all night. However, media coverage was mixed to say the least, with some newspapers continuing to imagine "no-holds-barred" and "bare-knuckle" bouts in poison ink articles.

Franklin and Silva rewarded the fans with a terrific bout, with ex-high school teacher Franklin just about getting the higher percentages to earn a decision. Also on the historic card, future UFC heavyweight champion Cain Velasquez overcame the fearsome striking of Cheick Kongo in the first major test of his young career.

Dennis Siver may be quietly spoken but he is an explosive UFC talent.

Astonishingly, Velasquez was almost inconsolable after the fight, feeling he had performed well below his capabilities despite dominating the fight 30-27 on all three judges' scorecards. UFC President Dana White vehemently disagreed, saying that the Mexican-American proved his chin and heart.

Also on the card, the improving Russian-German lightweight Dennis Siver subbed Dale Hartt in the first round to send the local fans ballistic.

Siver again demonstrated his rear-naked choke when the UFC returned to Germany the following year with November 2010's UFC 122, this time taking full advantage of a rocked Andre Winner inside four minutes. This time Siver was joined by German debutant Pascal Krauss, who also beat a Briton at UFC 122, outpointing Mark Scanlon in the fight of the night.

In the headline fight of the 10-fight card, which took place at the König Pilsener Arena, Oberhausen, Yushin Okami defeated Nate Marquardt to earn his shot at Anderson Silva's UFC middleweight championship.

Asked about the continued refusal of sections of the German establishment to accept the reality of the MMA as a sport, Dana White said: "It doesn't bother us. We couldn't get into Ontario, Canada, and we opened an office there. We can't get into New York right now, as crazy as that is. But this thing isn't going away. The German fans want us here and we want to be here."

UFC IN THE UAE

Abu Dhabi is synonymous among MMA hardcores with the world's premier BJJ tournament and, lately, with the UFC.

Desert shocker—Frankie Edgar would defeat BJ Penn at UFC 112.

The name of the capital of the United Arab Emirates has long been part of the mixed martial arts fan's vocabulary. UFC fans all over the world have heard the term "Abu Dhabi Champion" or "high-level Abu Dhabi BJJ" applied to the likes of Diego Sanchez, Fabricio Werdum, Gunnar Nelson and Demian Maia, after these UFC fighters and more had competed in the Abu Dhabi Combat Club Submission Wrestling World Championship.

With so many MMA fighters competing in the ADCC Championships, Abu Dhabi had already become part of MMA lore when it was announced that Abu Dhabi's Flash Entertainment had purchased 10 percent of the UFC in January 2010.

UFC Chairman Lorenzo Fertitta said: "Over the past few years, we have built a relationship with all levels of the Flash organization. They share our vision, passion, and enthusiasm for the UFC. We are confident that this partnership will accelerate the worldwide growth of the UFC."

"Accelerated" does not do justice to the speed in which the UFC's inaugural event in the UAE was put together. Within three months of the Flash, the UFC had landed in the Middle East for the first time.

UFC 112: Invincible took place in a specially constructed outdoor arena on Yas Island, Abu Dhabi, on April 10, 2010. The 10,000-seat venue was built over the course of two months in between the Ferrari World theme park and Formula 1 motor racing circuit on what is, astonishingly, a man-made island featuring hotels and other attractions constructed to the cost of some $36 billion.

"We don't have a Plan B if it rains," joked Dana White in the days leading up to the event, knowing that the chance of any rainfall in April in the UAE was anorexically slender. "But we are obviously taking precautions by covering up the Octagon canvas until the last minute before the show."

Nevertheless, the actual lettering on the Octagon ringposts literally melted off in the searing desert heat and had to be replaced when the sun began to cool in the early evening.

The desert night sky and unique setting inspired Frankie Edgar, a 5-1 challenger to lightweight champion BJ Penn, to pull off the upset of the year and Renzo Gracie, an MMA legend and folk hero in Abu Dhabi, to put up sterling resistance against Matt Hughes.

Mark Munoz beat Kendall Grove in a UAE UFC thriller.

UFC IN JAPAN

The incredible boom of 1997 to 2005 is over, but the Land of the Rising Sun's place in mixed martial arts lore is secure.

Jiu-jitsu, kempo, karate, ninjustu, sumo, judo, the samurai, and ninja—Japan is the spiritual home of traditional martial arts. However, the Land of the Rising Sun has also played an instrumental role in modern MMA.

There were four UFC events in the space of three years from December 1997 to December 2000, the first being "Ultimate Japan", which took place in front of 5,000 fans at the Yokohama Arena, Yokohama.

As with so many of these early shows, the inaugural Japanese event featured many bouts which are now considered of historical significance: Randy Couture won his first UFC heavyweight title, Frank Shamrock won the UFC middleweight title, and—in a bizarre twist of fortune—Japanese wrestling star Kazushi Sakuraba rematched with Marcus Silveira just hours after going to a no-decision with the same man to win the four-man tournament. The bizarre happenstance, which occurred after the other semifinal bout saw both men unable to continue, was the birth of the "Saku" legend in Japan.

The second "Ultimate Japan"—UFC 23—is noteworthy only in that looking back the end of the UFC seemed inevitable. The card, which took place on November 19, 1999, in Toyko, featured the final one-night tournament in the UFC, a four-man event to crown a "UFC Japan" champion because the idea at the time was for UFC Japan to run separate events.

Four months later, at Ultimate Japan 3 in Tokyo, Tito Ortiz defeated Wanderlei Silva for the UFC light heavyweight title vacated by Frank Shamrock. The brash Ortiz would go on to reign for three and a half years, an overall record which would stand until Anderson Silva broke it recently.

UFC 29 was not only the most recent event in Japan, but the final event promoted by SEG, as 2001 would bring in a new era for the company and sport with the UFC's sale to Zuffa LLC. A largely unknown fighter named Chuck Liddell won the opening bout of the show, and as he celebrated, his manager, a man named Dana White, joined him in the Octagon. A month later, White was named UFC President. It would take Zuffa and White a decade to bring the Octagon back to Japan but, in January 2012, UFC 144 sold out the Saitama Super Arena. The UFC was finally back.

Japanese favorite Norifumi "Kid" Yamamoto weighs in for UFC 126 debut.

Yushin Okami—more UFC wins than any other Japanese fighter.

UFC IN AUSTRALIA

It's a long way to go for a fight, but the passionate Australian fans make the trip worth it.

Inspired by the early UFCs, small hall Australian MMA shows began popping up within a couple of years of the Royce Gracie-led revolution. Home-grown wrestling talents like Chris "The Hammer" Haseman began experimenting in boxing and rudimentary submissions and an Aussie—Elvis Sinosic—challenged for the UFC light heavyweight title (vs. Tito Ortiz) as early as 2001.

So perhaps it shouldn't have come as that much of a surprise when the UFC's popularity Down Under simply exploded in 2009.

However, few expected the company's first ever show in Australia, February 2010's UFC 110, to sell out the 18,000-seat Acer Arena in Sydney within two hours.

But such was the demand for tickets to see a card stacked with the likes of Cain Velasquez vs. Minotauro Nogueira and Wanderlei Silva vs. Michael Bisping, a 500-seat overspill venue was set up next door.

The emotional highlight of the UFC's first trip Down Under was local BJJ specialist George Sotiropoulos' stunning rout of the much-favored Joe Stevenson over three exciting rounds. "G-Sot" had left Australia years before, against his family and friends' best advice, to pursue his dream of UFC glory and his return home could not have been more triumphant.

And in the main event, Cain came of age by obliterating Nogueira inside 150 seconds to earn his UFC heavyweight title shot later in the year. With the media and wider public embracing the sport, it wasn't long before plans were drawn up for the UFC to return to the Harbor City.

"Actually, the Octagon never left," said Dana White. "It takes over four months on a boat to ship it from Europe or the US, so we left an Octagon in storage in Sydney."

Four more hugely successful shows have already followed, and an Australia vs UK season of *The Ultimate Fighter* provided a smash hit. Plus, 2013's *The Ultimate Fighter: Nations* features an Australian team taking on a Canadian squad.

"Australia is blowing up for the UFC," White added in a rare understatement.

Sydney's James Te Huna scores a UFC 110 slam.

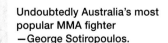

Undoubtedly Australia's most popular MMA fighter —George Sotiropoulos.

TITLE LINEAGE

The early years of the UFC saw a series of one-night tournaments, Super Fights, and no weight classes. But in 1997, a new era began with the crowning of the UFC's first world champion.

After existing in a Wild West of sorts, with fighters sometimes forced to give up 50 to 100lb in a fight, the UFC instituted two weight classes—heavyweight (200lb and over) and lightweight (199lb and under)—at UFC 12. In that event, on February 7, 1997, unbeaten Mark Coleman defeated Dan Severn to win the organization's first divisional championship.

There would be more changes in the coming years, with additional weight classes slowly being implemented in the interests of safety and fair competition. By UFC 31 in 2001, the divisions that exist today were in place for the first time.

During this early championship era, there were few dominant champions with the exception of Frank Shamrock, Pat Miletich, and Matt Hughes, and with the UFC in a precarious position until Zuffa arrived to begin steadying the sinking ship, fighters followed the dollar wherever it went, leaving titles vacant in several instances. It wasn't until a solid business model allowed fighters to make a full-time wage as pro athletes that stability came to each division in the UFC.

UFC 1–45

- **Mark Coleman**—defeats Dan Severn at UFC 12 (2/7/97) to become the first UFC heavyweight champion.
- **Maurice Smith**—defeats Coleman at UFC 14 (7/27/97).
- **Randy Couture**—defeats Smith at Ultimate Japan (12/21/97). Couture vacates his title after a contract dispute with the UFC.
- **Bas Rutten**—defeats Kevin Randleman at UFC 20 (5/7/99) to win the vacant title. Rutten vacates the title.
- **Kevin Randleman**—defeats Pete Williams at UFC 23 (11/19/99) to win the vacant title.
- **Randy Couture**—returns to the UFC and regains his title by defeating Randleman at UFC 28 (11/17/00).
- **Josh Barnett**—defeats Couture at UFC 36 (3/22/02) to win the title. Barnett loses his belt after testing positive for steroids.
- **Ricco Rodriguez**—defeats Couture at UFC 39 (9/27/02) to claim the vacant crown.
- **Tim Sylvia**—stops Rodriguez at UFC 41 (2/28/03) to become champion. Sylvia relinquishes his crown after testing positive for steroids following his first title defense against Gan McGee.

Randy Couture defeats Maurice Smith to take the UFC Heavyweight Championship at the Yokohama Arena, Japan, in 1997.

LIGHT HEAVYWEIGHT (205lb)

- **Frank Shamrock**—defeats Kevin Jackson at Ultimate Japan (12/21/97) to become the first UFC light heavyweight champion. The title was then called the middleweight title. He retires from the UFC in November of 1999, vacating the title.
- **Tito Ortiz**—defeats Wanderlei Silva at UFC 25 (4/14/00) to win the vacant title. After a period of inactivity in 2003, Chuck Liddell and Randy Couture are selected to fight for an interim title.
- **Randy Couture**—defeats Chuck Liddell at UFC 43 (6/6/03) for the interim title. He defeats Ortiz at UFC 44 (9/26/03) to claim the undisputed crown.

Tito Ortiz gets the verdict over Wanderlei Silva at the headline event of UFC 25.

MIDDLEWEIGHT (185lb)

- **Dave Menne**—defeats Gil Castillo at UFC 33 (9/28/01) to win the first UFC middleweight championship.
- **Murilo Bustamante**—defeats Menne at UFC 35 (1/11/02) to win the title. Bustamante vacates the title after one defense and leaves the organization.

WELTERWEIGHT (170lb)

- **Pat Miletich**—defeats Mikey Burnett at UFC Brazil (10/16/98) to win the UFC welterweight title, which was then called the lightweight title.
- **Carlos Newton**—defeats Miletich at UFC 31 (5/4/01) to win the title.
- **Matt Hughes**—defeats Newton at UFC 34 (11/2/01) to win the title.

LIGHTWEIGHT (155lb)

Jens Pulver—defeats Caol Uno at UFC 30 (2/23/01) to win the UFC lightweight championship, which was then called the bantamweight title. Pulver defended the title twice before leaving the organization and vacating the title. In 2002–03, a four-man tournament featuring BJ Penn, Caol Uno, Matt Serra, and Din Thomas was held to determine a new champion, but the title remained vacant after a five-round draw between Penn and Uno in the final at UFC 41.

After a rough start, the champions of the UFC began delivering the fights combat sports fans expected from their titleholders. In the process, a new age dawned in the fastest-growing sport in the world.

By the time UFC 46 kicked off in 2004, the sport of mixed martial arts was on the verge of a mainstream breakthrough that would be spearheaded in 2005 by the first season of *The Ultimate Fighter* and the epic finale between Forest Griffin and Stephan Bonnar.

In the championship ranks, the heavyweights and light heavyweights routinely swapped title belts. What had happened was that the level of competition had got to such a height that any fighter could beat any other on any given night.

And during this launch of a Golden Age in the sport, three dominant champions emerged in the form of Anderson Silva, Georges St-Pierre, and BJ Penn.

HEAVYWEIGHT (Over 205lb)

- **Frank Mir**—defeats Tim Sylvia for the vacant title at UFC 48 (6/19/04). Mir is seriously injured in a motorcycle accident and forced to give up his belt while he recovers from his injuries.
- **Andrei Arlovski**—defeats Sylvia at UFC 51 (2/5/05) to claim the interim title, which is later upgraded to the full championship.
- **Tim Sylvia**—becomes only the second man to regain the heavyweight championship when he defeats Arlovski at UFC 59 (4/15/06).
- **Randy Couture**—becomes the first man to win the heavyweight title three times when he beats Sylvia at UFC 68 (3/3/07). After a period of inactivity, Minotauro Nogueira and Tim Sylvia are selected to fight for the interim title. Couture subsequently returns to active status in November of 2008.
- **Minotauro Nogueira**—defeats Sylvia to win the interim heavyweight championship at UFC 81 (2/2/08).
- **Frank Mir**—defeats Nogueira at UFC 92 (12/27/08) to win the interim heavyweight championship.
- **Brock Lesnar**—defeats Couture at UFC 91 (11/15/08) to win the UFC heavyweight title.

Rashad Evans lands some brutal blows to Forrest Griffin to win his first championship.

- **Vitor Belfort**—defeats Couture at UFC 46 (1/31/04) to win the title.
- **Randy Couture**—regains the championship by defeating Belfort at UFC 49 (8/21/04).
- **Chuck Liddell**—wins the light heavyweight title by defeating Couture at UFC 52 (4/16/05).
- **Quinton Jackson**—wins the light heavyweight title by defeating Liddell at UFC 71 (5/26/07).
- **Forrest Griffin**—wins the light heavyweight title by decisioning Jackson at UFC 86 (7/5/08).
- **Rashad Evans**—wins the light heavyweight title with a defeat of Griffin at UFC 92 (12/27/08).

MIDDLEWEIGHT (185lb)

- **Evan Tanner**—defeats David Terrell at UFC 51 (2/5/05) to win the vacant middleweight title.
- **Rich Franklin**—defeats Tanner at UFC 53 (6/4/05) to win the title.
- **Anderson Silva**—defeats Franklin at UFC 64 (10/14/06) to win the title.

After a devastating head kick and landing multiple knees in the clinch, Anderson Silva defeated Rich Franklin by a knockout in round one at UFC 64.

- **BJ Penn**—defeats Hughes at UFC 46 (1/31/04) to win the welterweight championship. Penn subsequently leaves the organization, rendering the title vacant.
- **Matt Hughes**—regains the championship by defeating Georges St-Pierre at UFC 50 (10/22/04) to win the vacant title.
- **Georges St-Pierre**—defeats Hughes at UFC 65 (11/18/06) to win the championship.
- **Matt Serra**—stops St-Pierre at UFC 69 (4/7/07) to win the title. An injury to Serra forces an interim title bout between St-Pierre and Hughes.
- **Georges St-Pierre**—wins interim title with a win over Hughes at UFC 79 (12/29/07). Regains the undisputed title by stopping Serra at UFC 83 (4/19/08).

LIGHTWEIGHT (155lb)

After the Penn–Uno II draw, the division is used sporadically until the UFC 49 bout between Yves Edwards and Josh Thomson in 2004. The weight class does not return until UFC 58 in 2006.

- **Sean Sherk**—defeats Kenny Florian at UFC 64 (10/14/06) to win the vacant UFC lightweight title. Defends title against Hermes Franca but is subsequently stripped of the belt after testing positive for steroids.
- **BJ Penn**—defeats Joe Stevenson in the second round at UFC 80 (1/19/08) to win the vacant UFC lightweight crown.

Today's UFC champions—Velasquez, Jones, Weidman, St-Pierre, Henderson, Aldo, Cruz and Johnson—have become household names, a testament not only to their talent and memorable fights, but to the growth of the sport worldwide.

The modern era's championship bouts have been some of the best in UFC history, and as far as the champions go, we've seen dominant titleholders extending their reigns, young guns making their mark at the top, and everything in between.

Plus, with three new weight classes – flyweight, bantamweight, featherweight – and a women's bantamweight division, the best is yet to come for fight fans.

Georges St-Pierre's improved wrestling kept Matt Hughes at bay, and the Canadian took the belt with his superior striking.

HEAVYWEIGHT (Over 205lb)

- **Brock Lesnar**—a serious illness sidelines Lesnar, causing an interim heavyweight title bout to be scheduled between Shane Carwin and Frank Mir at UFC 111 in 2010. Lesnar returns and defeats the winner of that fight, Carwin, to unify the belts once again.
- **Shane Carwin**—defeats Frank Mir via a first-round KO at UFC 111 (3/27/10) to win interim title. Loses to Lesnar via second-round submission at UFC 116.
- **Cain Velasquez**—defeats Brock Lesnar at UFC 121 (10/23/10) to win the UFC heavyweight title. Lost to Junior dos Santos at UFC on Fox1.

- **Junior dos Santos (2011-12)**—defeats Cain Velasquez via KO in the first round at UFC on FOX 1 (11/12/11) to win the UFC heavyweight title. Defended title against Frank Mir. Lost title to Cain Velasquez at UFC 155.
- **Cain Velasquez (2012 -)**—defeats Junior dos Santos via five round unanimous decision at UFC 155 (12/29/12) to regain the heavyweight title. Defended title against Antonio Silva.

LIGHT HEAVYWEIGHT (205lb)

- **Lyoto Machida**—wins the light heavyweight title with a second-round KO of Rashad Evans at UFC 98 (5/23/09). Defended the title against Mauricio Rua. Lost title to Rua at UFC 113.
- **Mauricio Rua**—wins the light heavyweight title with a first round KO of Lyoto Machida at UFC 113 (5/8/10). Lost title to Jon Jones at UFC 128.
- **Jon Jones**—wins the light heavyweight title with a third round TKO of Mauricio Rua at UFC 128 (3/19/11). Defended the title against Quinton Jackson, Lyoto Machida, Rashad Evans, Vitor Belfort, and Chael Sonnen.

Jon Jones punches Mauricio 'Shogun' Rua during his successful challenge for the light heavyweight championship belt at UFC 128.

MIDDLEWEIGHT (185lb)

- **Anderson Silva**—defeats Rich Franklin at UFC 64 (10/14/06) to win the title. Silva defeats Travis Lutter in what should have been his first title defense, but Lutter came in overweight, rendering the bout a non-title affair. Silva defended the belt against Nate Marquardt, Franklin, Henderson, Patrick Cote, Thales Leites, Demian Maia, Chael Sonnen (twice), Vitor Belfort, and Yushin Okami. Lost title to Chris Weidman at UFC 162 (7/6/13).
- **Chris Weidman**—defeats Anderson Silva at UFC 163 (7/6/13) to win title.

WELTERWEIGHT (170lb)

- **Georges St-Pierre**—Wins interim title with win over Hughes at UFC 79. Regains the undisputed title by stopping Serra in the second round at UFC 83 (4/19/08). GSP has defended his title against Jon Fitch, BJ Penn, Thiago Alves, Dan Hardy, Josh Koscheck, Jake Shields, Carlos Condit, and Nick Diaz.

- **Carlos Condit**—Won interim title with win over Nick Diaz at UFC 143. Lost belt in unification fight with St-Pierre at UFC 154 (11/17/12).

LIGHTWEIGHT (155lb)

- **Frankie Edgar**—defeats BJ Penn via unanimous decision at UFC 112 (4/10/10) to win the UFC crown. Edgar defended the title against Penn (W5), and Maynard (Draw5 and KO4).

- **Benson Henderson**—defeats Frankie Edgar via unanimous decision at UFC 144 (2/26/12) to win the UFC crown. Has defended title against Edgar, Nate Diaz, and Gilbert Melendez.

FEATHERWEIGHT (145lb)

- **Jose Aldo**—Declared first UFC Featherweight Champion after WEC / UFC merger in 2010. Awarded belt before UFC 123 in November of 2010. Defended title successfully against Mark Hominick, Kenny Florian, Chad Mendes, Frankie Edgar, and Chan Sung Jung.

BANTAMWEIGHT (135lb)

- **Dominick Cruz**—WEC bantamweight champion who defeated Scott Jorgensen at WEC 53 on December 16, 2010 to win first UFC Bantamweight Championship. Defended title successfully against Urijah Faber and Demetrious Johnson.

- **Renan Barao**—Won interim UFC bantamweight title by defeating Urijah Faber at UFC 149 (7/21/12). Defended title against Michael McDonald.

FLYWEIGHT (125lb)

- **Demetrious Johnson**—Won vacant UFC flyweight title by defeating Joseph Benavidez at UFC 152 (9/22/12). Defended title against John Dodson and John Moraga.

WOMEN'S BANTAMWEIGHT (135lb)

- **Ronda Rousey**—Named UFC women's bantamweight champion in December of 2012. Defended title against Liz Carmouche.

TOP 10 UFC
MOMENTS

There have been more than 250 UFC events and more than 2,500 fights since the organization began in 1993, and every single one is part of the history of the sport. Some moments, though, are indelibly etched into the annals of time...

Brock Lesnar reacts after his second-round-submission win over Shane Carwin at UFC 116.

The Beginning

UFC 1 Held on November 12, 1993, in Denver, Colorado, the first Ultimate Fighting Championship event—which was supposedly a one-off tournament billed as "no-holds-barred" fighting— forever changed the way martial arts is viewed.

The inaugural UFC event was designed to answer the age-old question of what form of combat, be it boxing, wrestling, karate, kung-fu or anything else, was the "'ultimate" style. It was also created to introduce an American audience to a new martial art which would become known as "Brazilian Jiu-Jitsu."

The Gracie family were already urban legends in their native land, and Royce Gracie was selected by the clan to enter the one-night tournament, which also featured boxer Art Jimmerson, sumo fighter Teila Tuli, taekwondo champion Patrick Smith, kickboxers Kevin Rosier, Gerard Gordeau, and Zane Frazier, and Pancrase veteran Ken Shamrock.

Even the organizers didn't know what to expect, but the Gracies did. Despite giving up an astonishing 180lb in one fight, the undersized Royce effortlessly defeated three opponents—all from fighting off his back— exposing centuries of fighting clichés as worthless. The martial arts changed more that one night than in the previous century.

The poster for the original UFC event.

Liddell makes debut

UFC 17 Some Octagon moments come and go with seemingly little hint of their future significance to the sport. So it was at UFC 17, when an unheralded striker named Charles David Liddell appeared in the first bout of the night.

UFC 17: Redemption took place at the Mobile Civic Center, in Mobile, Alabama, on May 15, 1998. The UFC was beginning to struggle, financially, and the dark days of being off Pay-Per-View were drawing in. However, the show remains notable for several reasons. It was the second to last time the UFC would run a one-night elimination tournament (the last being UFC 23), and it featured the debuts of future UFC champions Dan Henderson and Carlos Newton.

But the real footnote in history was that future UFC Hall of Famer Chuck "The Iceman" Liddell made his UFC debut in an untelevised bout against a half-forgotten fighter named Noe Hernandez. And, although he was taken the distance on this occasion, Liddell would go on to knock out a total of 10 opponents in the UFC, five of them being in UFC light heavyweight title fights, a record which stands to this day.

The Ice Age began at UFC 17.

Chuck "The Iceman" Liddell went on to become a UFC Hall of Famer.

Zuffa buys the UFC

The story has already passed into urban legend: promoted as a spectacle rather than a sport, the UFC had been driven off Pay-Per-View, and was done, finished. Then two childhood friends had an idea…

In late 2000 a Las Vegas boxing gym owner and manager named Dana White was representing his friend Chuck Liddell in negotiations with the UFC's original owners. He learned that not only couldn't the UFC pay his clients bigger purses but, in fact, it was actually close to going under.

White made a call to high school friend Lorenzo Fertitta, who along with brother Frank was a Las Vegas businessman and lifelong fight fan. In January 2001, the newly formed Zuffa LLC bought the UFC and, with White installed as the new UFC President, Zuffa began to transform the UFC into a highly organized sport.

"Lorenzo, Frank and I always felt that you'd watch a spectacle once, but that this wasn't a spectacle. Instead of running away from regulations we ran towards it," Said White. "It is a sport—and we knew we could make it the biggest sport in the world."

A man on a mission: UFC President Dana White.

UFC makes Las Vegas debut

UFC 33 On September 28, 2001 the UFC finally debuted in the city dubbed the Fight Capital of the World.

Las Vegas's most famous moniker may well be "Sin City," but the Nevada resorts' long history of hosting the biggest boxing matches have also earned it the nickname "Fight Town." Yet, as it approached the eighth anniversary of its inception, the UFC had yet to stage a single bout in Vegas.

That changed on September 28, 2001, when UFC 33 rocked the Mandalay Bay Events Center. Just over 9,500 fans were on hand to see three title bouts: Tito Ortiz defended his 205lb belt against Vladimir Matyushenko, lightweight king Jens Pulver beat Dennis Hallman and Dave Menne outpointed Gil Castillo to become the first ever middleweight champ.

While UFC 33 doesn't threaten the likes of UFC 116 as the most exciting card ever, as the first event to be sanctioned by the world-renowned Nevada State Athletic Commission, it has its place in history.

The UFC finally debuts in the world fight capital, Las Vegas.

The Brawl at the Hall: the UFC lands in England

UFC 38 Zuffa always believed the UFC was a truly international sport, and in the summer of 2002 less than 18 months after buying the company, it took the Octagon across the Atlantic to London, for an historic first.

"When we first bought this company," President Dana White said, "we knew this thing would work in the UK. The UK pretty much invented modern boxing and they like fighting, so it was a no-brainer to go there."

The first incursion on to British soil came on July 13, 2002, at the oval-shaped arena which was opened by Queen Victoria in 1871. The event sold out and as well as laying the foundations for a permanent office in London, it was at UFC 38 that Matt Hughes cemented his status as a welterweight legend, when he easily defeated Carlos Newton in their rematch.

But for the local fans, the night belonged to English heavyweight Ian Freeman, who upset champion-in-waiting Frank Mir despite a heartbreaking family tragedy. Freeman's father had passed away before the fight, and his family had made the decision not to tell "The Machine" until after the bout.

Historic setting, historic show... UFC 38 was held at London's Royal Albert Hall.

Ronda Rousey and Liz Carmouche make history

Ronda Rousey grounds and pounds Liz Carmouche at UFC 157.

UFC 157 For years, Dana White had insisted that women would "never" compete in the UFC. But the incredible talents of Ronda Rousey, Liz Carmouche, Miesha Tate and others would not be denied.

The March 2012 women's bantamweight title fight between champ Miesha Tate and brash, unbeaten challenger Ronda Rousey changed everything for women's MMA.

At ringside for only the third time at an event promoted by the UFC's now defunct sister organization Strikeforce, Dana White was blown away, not only by the seemingly irrepressible Rousey but also Tate's astonishing bravery in refusing to submit to one of the most painful-looking armbars in the sport's history.

White's mind had been changed. Less than a year later, Strikeforce was folded into the UFC, and Rousey was named the first UFC women's bantamweight champion. "Rowdy" made her first defense in the main event of February 2013's UFC 157 in Anaheim, California. After a blaze of unprecedented publicity, Rousey defeated Liz Carmouche via trademark armbar in a stirring one-round fight.

Jon Jones – UFC crime fighter

UFC 128 On the day of their first UFC title shot, most fighters would try to sleep in, or relax playing video games or watching movies in their hotel rooms. Jon Jones fights crime.

Jon Jones just wanted to visit a local park to clear his mind before his UFC 128 light heavyweight title challenge against Shogun Rua in Newark, New Jersey, on March 19, 2011. What followed is so incredible it should be read in Jones' own words.

He said: "We heard a lady screaming she'd been mugged. Some thief had stolen her stuff. My camp told me not to go after the guy but I did anyway. We chased after this guy, I tripped him, and we held him down until the cops arrived. I gave the lady her stuff back and she said it was karma and I would win the title that night."

Karma may have helped, but it was Jones' astonishing speed and talent which defeated Rua later that night.

"I don't know what else he's doing today," Dana White joked, "maybe delivering a baby on the way out of the arena."

Just 23, Jon Jones became the youngest UFC champion in history on March 19, 2011.

"In a lot of ways I felt as if I was a champion just because of the way I carry myself as a person and the way I look at life. And even before I got the belt I felt like I was an elite fighter in the world."
Jon Jones

Reality TV saves the UFC

Despite Zuffa's best efforts, the UFC still hadn't caught the imagination of the mainstream as 2005 dawned. Then the company rolled the dice by spending $10 million on a reality TV series…

Dana White freely admits the UFC was struggling to the point where he and his partners considered selling it. He said, "People weren't giving this sport a chance. Eventually we sat down and came up with a Trojan horse; we'd get people watching the UFC without even realizing it."

The Trojan horse was *The Ultimate Fighter*, a reality TV series where 16 of the best unsigned fighters would live and train together and, coached by a pair of UFC legends, compete for a six-figure UFC contract.

TUF, as it was affectionately dubbed, was an international sensation. Viewers got to see – for the first time – just what makes this sport so great: the courage, hard work, sacrifice, and unparalleled athleticism. A new generation of fans was converted.

The show ushered in the new era of mainstream MMA and its popularity continues to soar. The U.S.-based show is currently in its 18th season, and there have already been international editions in Australia, Canada and Brazil.

Some rare downtime on the set of the show that brought the UFC to the next level.

UFC leaps into the mainstream

The explosion in popularity between 2005 and 2010 earned the UFC the title "the fastest growing sport in the world," but some argue the plunge into the mainstream really came in 2011.

By the end of 2010, the UFC had long since supplanted boxing as the combat sport of a new generation, but Zuffa never measured its success against the sweet science.

"We want to make this the biggest sport of the world," Dana White said. "People laugh, but this is going to be bigger than soccer, bigger than everything."

White's dream looked a while lot less fanciful during the summer of 2011, when the UFC announced a landmark seven-year deal with the FOX family. For the very first time, the UFC would show fights on network TV in the United States, reaching the same mainstream audiences as sports like the NFL enjoyed.

The first UFC event on FOX drew over 9.2 million viewers in the U.S.

"This is a game-changer," White said. "We've always wanted to get in network TV but only with the right people. These guys are so smart, such great partners… we couldn't be more excited. Everyone in America can now see how awesome the UFC is."

UFC draws 55,724 fans to Rogers Centre

UFC 129 In by far the largest attendance for a MMA event in the sport's young history, 55,724 fans jam-packed the famous Rogers Centre in Toronto, Canada, for an unforgettable night.

Perhaps more than any major sports promoter, Dana White and the UFC believe the ticket-buying audience should have the greatest experience possible. Every single seat at a UFC event has an unobstructed sight-line and, in what other combat sports would consider a near-sacrilegious policy, the UFC actually "kills" seats in order to hang the giant screens fans refer to when fights hit the ground.

For those reasons, White resisted the idea of running a UFC event in a stadium or outdoor arena even when the demand was clearly there. But, when the Providential Government finally began regulating MMA on January 1, 2011, the UFC took a serious look at the historic Rogers Centre, a stunning but huge facility in downtown Toronto.

UFC 129 was witnessed by 55,724 fans at Toronto's Rogers Centre.

Working with the team at the venue, the UFC was satisfied that the UFC experience could actually be augmented at Rogers. The company's faith was rewarded by a jaw-dropping instantaneous sell-out and vintage performances by world champions Georges St-Pierre and Jose Aldo.

A DAY IN THE LIFE
OF A UFC FIGHTER

If there's one thing you can say about a day in the life of a UFC fighter, it's that it's far from typical. In fact, it's different for every athlete who steps into the Octagon, and depends a lot on mood, personality, sleep patterns, and their lives outside of competition.

Some fighters like to sleep in late and train deep into the night. Others are family men, so they're up at the crack of dawn to get some roadwork in before getting their kids to school. But if they do share one thing in common, it's the desire to be the best, and that means some long hours in the gym.

For younger fighters who are newer to the game, training usually involves what they've always worked on, which is all aspects of mixed martial arts. This new breed of MMA fighter is characterized by guys like Georges St-Pierre and Jon Jones, who didn't come into the sport with just one discipline, adding the rest as they went along. They practically learned everything at once, and their dynamic styles reflect that.

For veterans like former UFC lightweight champion Jens Pulver, being in the game these days means working even harder to keep up, but "Lil' Evil" likes that kind of challenge, as he pointed out before his WEC debut in 2007.

"At one point, after you've been fighting a while, you lose the desire to drill and learn something new. And somewhere along the line, the sport passed me up in the aspect of 'here are all these young guys, they're hungry, they've got well-rounded ground games, they've got good standup games, and they're in shape.' So now I'm having fun learning again and starting over."

Another daily requirement if you're a high-profile fighter in the UFC is a host of media obligations. Some fighters embrace the opportunity to get their story out to the world, while others are a bit more shy. But no matter what your personality, getting yourself in front of the public and promoting your fight is a necessity. And for main eventers, the ante gets raised even higher and usually involves pre-fight press conferences and a teleconference with the worldwide media. UFC lightweight champion Frankie Edgar discussed his media schedule before his UFC 125 bout against Gray Maynard, and by this time, he was an old pro.

"This being my third title fight, it was the third conference call I did, and I'm getting more accustomed to them," he said. "When it comes to scheduling all the other interviews I play it by ear. My schedule shifts

Kurt Pellegrino and Fabricio Camoes square off at the weigh-in of their UFC 111 bout.

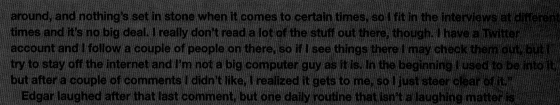
around, and nothing's set in stone when it comes to certain times, so I fit in the interviews at different times and it's no big deal. I really don't read a lot of the stuff out there, though. I have a Twitter account and I follow a couple of people on there, so if I see things there I may check them out, but I try to stay off the internet and I'm not a big computer guy as it is. In the beginning I used to be into it, but after a couple of comments I didn't like, I realized it gets to me, so I just steer clear of it."

Edgar laughed after that last comment, but one daily routine that isn't a laughing matter is watching your weight. This becomes a truly stressful event on weigh-in day, but again, if you're a veteran of the sport, you become used to it, especially if you're a wrestler like former UFC light heavyweight champion Rashad Evans.

"Weigh-in day is the calm before the storm," he said. "After I wake up, [UFC site coordinator] Burt [Watson] tells me what I've got to do and where I've got to meet for the pre-weigh-ins. After that, I cut weight, and after the weigh-in, I get together with my family and my coaching staff, and we have a dinner. As far as weight cutting goes, I've been used to cutting weight my whole life, since I come from a wrestling background. It's just water-weight, so it's pretty easy to lose once you know how to do it."

Easy for him to say, but that's like anything to do with the warriors of the Octagon. They make it look easy on fight night, but that's because the hard work has already been done in the gym in the weeks leading up to the bout. And that may be the only typical thing about a day in the life of a UFC fighter.

All the hard training comes down to this —15 or 25 minutes of battle in the Octagon.

UFC lightweight Dennis Siver speaks at a post-fight press conference following his win over Matt Wiman at UFC 132.

UFC
CLASSIC
FIGHTS

There have been so many great
fights in the history of the UFC,
but only a select few were
good enough to make this list.
Here are the best of the best.

It was an all-out war when "The Iceman" met "The Axe Murderer" at UFC 79.

FORREST GRIFFIN VS. STEPHAN BONNAR I

Griffin and Bonnar go to war in what UFC President Dana White calls the most important fight in UFC history.

Since forming parent company Zuffa LLC and becoming UFC President in January 2001, Dana White has attended over 130 UFC events and sat ringside for well over 1,250 UFC bouts, but he never hesitates when asked which is the most important fight he's ever promoted: the first ever *Ultimate Fighter* Finale showdown between light heavyweights Forrest Griffin and Stephan Bonnar.

So much was riding on the *TUF* Finale, which was held at the Cox Pavilion, Las Vegas, on April 9, 2005. The reality TV series had drawn a record television audience, but these curious newcomers would certainly tune out—perhaps forever—unless they saw something exciting on their TVs that night.

"*The Ultimate Fighter* was our Trojan Horse," White would later recall. "We got people watching MMA who would never have dreamed of watching a fight, but because it was a reality series and they got to see how cool these guys are and how hard they had to train, they became invested in them. By the time the finale came along, we wanted these new fans to tune in to find out who was going to win the contract."

Tune in they did, and in record numbers. And they witnessed what UFC color commentator Joe Rogan felt confident enough after only one round to call "the Hagler vs. Hearns of MMA" (referring to the legendary 1980s clash between Marvin Hagler and Tommy Hearns, which fans consider the best boxing match of all time). Their hopes and dreams on the line, both Griffin and Bonnar attacked with relish in the opening stanza, with Griffin's low kicks perhaps giving him a slight edge in a frenetic five minutes.

Bonnar took over in the second, cutting his opponent's nose with straight punches and using a Thai clinch to great effect, smashing home several knees to the jaw. However, Griffin refused to wilt despite a pace which would exhaust a racehorse.

Everything was on the third, an astonishing round with both men firing everything they had at each other. Griffin was the more aggressive, hurling punches and kicks at Bonnar, but "The American Psycho" slammed home some powerful shots of his own. After another astonishing stanza, Griffin took 29-28 verdicts from all three judges.

But White was so ecstatic with the efforts of both men, he declared that there was no real loser and gave each of them a UFC contract.

"I'll never forget what these two guys did for this company," White said recently. "These two are like my kids. They will be part of the UFC forever."

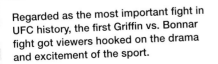

Regarded as the most important fight in UFC history, the first Griffin vs. Bonnar fight got viewers hooked on the drama and excitement of the sport.

ANDERSON SILVA VS. CHAEL SONNEN

In an incredible UFC encounter, Chael Sonnen proved that middleweight champion Silva was a) human after all and b) still almost impossible to defeat.

Initially considered by some to be nothing more than another number-one contender for the world's greatest mixed martial artist to dispatch with customary ease, by the time the Octagon door was locked at UFC 117, Chael Sonnen had everyone's full attention.

Sonnen was coming off two career-best wins over Yushin Okami and Nate Marquardt. However, it was the Oregon All-American's verbal assaults on Silva which turned the Oracle Arena in Oakland, California, into a cauldron.

Among the many outrageous comments Sonnen spouted were such zingers as "Anderson is no more the best fighter in the world than Big Foot is roaming the woods," "Anderson, you are going to be on your back more than a pornstar with a mortgage," and, perhaps most hurtfully to Silva, he said the champ's BJJ black belt from the Nogueira Brothers was as worthless as a Happy Meal toy.

Chael Sonnen shocked the world when he faced Anderson Silva in 2010, but he couldn't finish off the resilient "Spider."

Silva seethed silently at the disrespect shown to his mentors. "The Spider" literally wore his intentions as he stalked toward the Octagon: instead of the usual sponsored T-shirt he wore a full BJJ gi and the very black belt he had earned in the Nogueira dojo.

The fight was, to put it simply, jaw-dropping.

The challenger badly stunned Silva almost immediately before slamming the champion to the canvas and unleashing a fearful ground and pound attack. For four rounds Silva struggled to fend off the takedowns or get to his feet but, when he did, the Brazilian smashed home sickening strikes.

In the fifth, Sonnen's face was a mess but Silva was a mile behind on points. The challenger was two minutes away from the biggest upset in UFC history... and then a desperate Silva slapped on a triangle and forced an exhausted Sonnen to take.

The win spilled beyond clichés. To call it the greatest come from behind win in UFC history simply doesn't do Silva's victory justice.

"Nogueira jiu-jitsu!" the champ said, smiling through the pain.

"Anderson is no more the best fighter in the world than Big Foot is roaming the woods."
Chael Sonnen

MATT HUGHES VS. FRANK TRIGG II

In UFC President Dana White's favorite fight of all time, UFC welterweight king Hughes defeats nemesis Trigg in a bitter fight.

UFC welterweight king Matt Hughes went into his April 16, 2005 rematch with challenger Frank Trigg angry. The challenger had lost his previous title shot two years earlier, but had talked so much smack going into the UFC 52 rematch that Hughes was determined to obliterate Trigg so badly that he would never have to hear his name again.

The rematch lasted barely four minutes, but packed more drama into that single round than most fights could in five. After staring holes in each other's skulls before the opening horn, the pair traded punches evenly in the center of the Octagon until they locked up.

While pressing Hughes against the cage wall, Trigg caught the champion with a knee to the groin which went unnoticed by referee Mario Yamasaki. As Hughes retreated in agony, Trigg saw his chance and slammed home a left hook to the jaw which decked the champion.

In serious trouble, Hughes caught a flurry of blows on the ground as Trigg worked his way into full mount.

Hughes tried to escape but the challenger quickly capitalized with a rear naked choke. As the champ's face turned crimson the 14,562 fans at the Las Vegas MGM Grand sensed the title was moments away from changing due, in part, to a foul.

But amazingly former NCAA Division I standout Hughes powered out of the hold and then—somehow—picked Trigg up, ran across the Octagon with him and slammed him almost through the mat.

With Trigg in a daze it was now Hughes in control, and in the full mount he opened up on the New Yorker with both fists. With the packed house going wild, Trigg then turned and it was Hughes sinking in a rear naked choke, which produced a tap out at the 4:05 mark.

To this day, Dana White calls the bout his favorite, saying: "It was the most exciting comeback you will ever see. I was right there, Hughes was done. He got kneed low, then rocked badly by the punch and was turning red with the choke. But Matt Hughes showed why he's a Hall of Famer. He sucked it up and found a way to win. It was incredible."

Matt Hughes and Frank Trigg slug it out in the early going of their 2005 rematch.

Hughes delivers the slam that marked the beginning of the end for Trigg's title challenge.

CHUCK LIDDELL VS. WANDERLEI SILVA

A fight which took five years to make and almost didn't happen at all actually exceeded half a decade of expectations.

To newer fans, it seems impossible there was once another promotion which rivaled the UFC as the world's biggest combat sports organisation. But the Japanese-based PRIDE FC—which existed from 1997 to 2007—deserves its place in MMA history.

Perhaps the greatest PRIDE fighter of all—and certainly the most intimidating—was Brazilian striker Wanderlei Silva. His long reign of terror in PRIDE's version of the UFC's light heavyweight division saw him destroy fighters like Rampage Jackson (twice), Kazushi Sakuraba (three times), and Ricardo Arona.

Meanwhile, "The Iceman" Liddell was smashing the UFC's light heavyweight division like a wrecking ball, knocking out Randy Couture (twice), Tito Ortiz (twice), and Renato Sobral (twice). Fans spent hours on message boards arguing who was the greatest striker in the division and UFC President Dana White tried repeatedly to make the fight happen.

However, when the UFC bought PRIDE in 2007, all obstacles to the showdown were removed. The fight happened at the aptly entitled UFC 79: Nemesis on December 29, 2007, and despite fears both combatants were slightly past their best, the three-round war is indelibly etched into the hearts of MMA fans.

In a furnace-like Mandalay Bay Events Center, Liddell took the opening round, stunning "The Axe Murderer" with a right hand after countering a leg kick by Silva. However, while looking slightly the bigger puncher, Liddell was stung himself by one of Silva's infamously wild inside combinations toward the end of the round.

It was Silva who took the second round, one of the best in UFC history. Charging inside and tearing into Liddell with powerful hooks, Silva seemed to stun "The Iceman" on several occasions although, of course, Liddell fought fire with fire and cut his man with a right.

With everything riding on the last round, university graduate Liddell smartly changed things up and took Silva down. The former PRIDE champ got to his feet but soon ate a thunderous spinning backfist which badly hurt him. Another Liddell takedown towards the end of the round ensured "The Iceman" the "W."

Although he featured in three more huge fights, Liddell never tasted victory in the Octagon again. He'd burned the last ounce of his greatness in the furnace heat of the war with Silva.

> "I think the reason people like me is because I'll fight anybody, anywhere. I don't talk bad about people that don't deserve it."
> Chuck Liddell

This epic battle between "The Iceman" and "The Axe Murderer" was five years in the making but it didn't disappoint.

GEORGES ST-PIERRE VS. BJ PENN I

In one of the most debated decisions in the UFC's young history, two future Hall of Famers both believed they'd got the better of the other.

Going into UFC 58 in March 2006, BJ Penn had been away from the Octagon for two years due to a contractual dispute that had played out in public. The issues resolved, "The Prodigy" returned to the UFC's welterweight division to face red-hot contender Georges St-Pierre.

Penn had never lost the UFC welterweight title he had snatched from Matt Hughes inside the Octagon; he had been stripped of the belt during his extended hiatus from the organization. Penn and Hughes were anxious to get the rematch on and settle the identity of the real UFC champion.

But "GSP" had his own designs on the gold. The Canadian had emerged as a legitimate contender in Penn's absence and was already tagged as a "future great" by some more astute observers.

Penn could barely contain himself before the opening round, pacing back and forth and pushing at his gum-shield with his tongue. The pride of Hawaii bombed away from the get-go, but "GSP" kept calm in the eye of the storm.

This epic battle was so close that both fighters thought they has won.

A flurry by Penn bloodied "GSP"'s nose, which would drip crimson for the rest of the bout, and an accidental thumb to the eye had the Canadian seeing double. The pair exchanged sickening knees to the thighs and stomach along the fence but Penn fought off "GSP"'s takedown attempts and took the opener.

In the second, "GSP" began to find a home for his laser-guided punches and kicks, but Penn found a spot to land a big right which opened another cut, this time under "GSP"'s eye.

"GSP" fired back with strikes and—finally—completed the takedown. When Penn scrambled to his feet, he certainly landed the heavier shots, although "GSP" landed more often and with more variety.

How you scored the second was critical, though, because while Penn clearly had the best of the opener, the last round belonged to "GSP". St-Pierre made his stamina tell in the third by outstriking a tiring Penn. "GSP" then scored the takedown of the fight, scooping the smaller man up and slamming him to the mat. Two more takedowns followed, and Penn's own takedown attempt was stuffed.

After the horn, two judges scored it 29-28 for "GSP", with the third seeing it for Penn by the same margin.

BROCK LESNAR VS. FRANK MIR II

In the main event of the biggest UFC ever, UFC 100, Lesnar exacted his painful revenge upon nemesis Mir.

Held at the Mandalay Bay, Las Vegas, on July 11, 2009, UFC 100 was a celebration of what the UFC organization had become in the modern era of mixed martial arts. Having long since outgrown its niche roots as a curiosity or niche "extreme sport," the UFC proudly took its place among the world's most popular sports, commemorating its centenary event with a line-up featuring emerging stars, a battle of *TUF* coaches, and welterweight king Georges St-Pierre repelling the challenge of No.1 contender Thiago Alves.

However, the undisputed main event of the evening featured the culmination of the blood-feud between UFC heavyweight champion Brock Lesnar and interim champion Frank Mir.

The pair were unifying the championship which had temporarily become fragmented during reigning champion Randy Couture's extended hiatus from the UFC. An interim title had been created and Mir had knocked out the legendary Minotauro Nogueira to carry that belt into the UFC 100 bout, while Lesnar had stopped Couture for the linear title upon "The Natural"'s return to the UFC.

The clash was a rematch of the UFC 81 fight when Mir had to weather a brutal beating to crank in a kneebar on the hulking Lesnar in perhaps the most exciting one-round fight in the history of the heavyweight division.

In the following 17 months, the charismatic Mir repeatedly taunted the hot-headed Lesnar about the loss, and the bad blood reached boiling point during the build-up to the rematch at UFC 100.

At the first horn, former NCAA wrestling champ Lesnar once again took the BJJ master down, just as he had done in the original meeting. But this time it was different. Showing vast improvements in top control, the novice world champion used his wrestling and impossible physical strength to maul Mir, while his lunchbox-sized fists reduced the interim champ's features to mush.

The Las Vegan had bulked up for the bout, but his new muscles counted for naught against Lesnar's near-superhuman strength. After two rounds, the referee had seen enough and a fanatic Lesnar couldn't contain his excitement at exacting a painful reversal on the first man to defeat him.

"Talk some crap now!" Lesnar demanded of a still-dazed Mir.

"I told you—you had a lucky horseshoe up your ass, but I took it out and beat you over the head with it!"

It was an emotional ending to one of the biggest fights ever in combat sports.

Brock Lesnar got mad and got even in his rematch with Frank Mir at UFC 100.

MINOTAURO NOGUEIRA VS. RANDY COUTURE

Brazilian legend overcomes spirited challenge from "The Natural" to win one of the final PRIDE vs. UFC superfights.

In another dream fight made reality by the UFC's acquisition of PRIDE FC, former UFC heavyweight and light heavyweight champion Randy Couture and former PRIDE (and, by now, former UFC) champion Minotauro Nogueira finally squared off on August 29, 2009 at the Rose Garden in Portland, Oregon.

Although over a decade older at 46, Couture was considered the fresher fighter going into the fight, with Minotauro having labored somewhat in his previous few outings inside the Octagon. Couture wasted no time in testing that assessment, quickly slamming home several well-timed punches. The Brazilian pulled guard and deployed his BJJ mastery, but Couture's well-documented wrestling ability enabled him to quickly escape to his feet and begin to find a home for his fists once more.

Then suddenly Couture ate a huge right and was dropped to the canvas. "Big Nog" pounced on his fellow legend and sunk in a deep D'Arce choke. But, somehow, "The Natural" escaped and the battle was rejoined, to the delight of the 16,088 fans who attended UFC 102.

Both exchanged strikes on even terms, until Couture found his sweet-spot in the clinch and hammered home uppercuts from the "dirty boxing" stance. Although he had lost the round, the former Olympic alternate ended the first stanza in the ascendancy.

UFC Hall of Famer Couture again began faster in the second, although he ate some power shots before "Big Nog" took him down. It was clear the Brazilian intended to submit Couture, and indeed looked very close to doing just that when he synched in an arm-triangle. And yet, to the amazement of some, Couture's defensive jiu-jitsu was up to the task and he escaped several submission attempts from the man considered the best BJJ fighter in the history of the heavyweight division.

However, "Big Nog" also secured a full mount and clearly had the better of the second round.

The third stanza was a dogfight. Couture was dropped again by a right cross and spent the first half of the round getting grounded and pounded. However, with minutes left he reversed Nogueira and unloaded elbows that the late Evan Tanner would be proud of.

Nogueira earned a unanimous decision in a fight which will not soon be forgotten.

Legends collide in Portland as Randy Couture faces Minotauro Nogueira.

This classic encounter would eventually see Nogueira claim victory over Couture.

FRANKIE EDGAR VS. GRAY MAYNARD II

No one expected much in the way of fireworks from this New Year's Day rematch… but then the fists started flying.

In truth, Frankie "The Answer" Edgar's first defense of the UFC lightweight title was anticipated with mild intrigue rather than breathless excitement. True, the New Jersey boxer-wrestler was coming off two impressive title fight wins over the already legendary BJ Penn and was facing the one man to beat him—Gray "The Bully" Maynard—but the pair were a little too respectful to get the blood really pumping.

In fact Maynard, unbeaten in 11 fights going into the bout, didn't even seem to mind that it was Edgar —the same man whom he'd soundly outpointed three years earlier—who had gotten to fight Penn and not him. Nor did Edgar seem to particularly care that he simply wasn't getting the respect his wins over Penn rightly earned him.

Add to this overtly good-natured build-up the sense that the pair's wrestling-heavy styles simply didn't gel that well and the main event of UFC 125: Resolution wasn't the most eagerly awaited on the New Year's Day, 2011, card.

But Maynard savaged the champion at the opening horn, decking the shorter man three times in a wild first round which many referees would have stopped in favor of the challenger. Somehow, Edgar managed to keep in the fight, but he ate 47 power shots to the head in the first five minutes.

"The Answer" was still a little wobbly in the second but he astonishingly took the round, outboxing the challenger, who was clearly gassed from his first-round efforts. Edgar drew a roar from his supporters when he double-legged Maynard toward the end of the round.

The third round was fought on very even terms, with both lightweights landing great shots. Significantly, though, and unlike the first fight, Maynard was unable to take Edgar down at will. Edgar landed a big right, but "The Bully" blasted back and scored a takedown toward the end of the round.

The fourth round saw Edgar again do the better work with his jab, while the fifth probably belonged to Maynard's heavier power punches, although it was very close.

After an absolute classic Fight of the Night the judges rendered a split draw verdict.

Both men were crestfallen by the verdict but, in the cold light of day, it was the fairest result for what was a "Fight of the Year" candidate barely 22 hours into 2011.

> *"I kinda punched myself out in the first. I thought I won (rounds) 1, 3, 5. It was a close one, but I thought I won."*
> Gray Maynard

Maynard and Edgar contested an incredibly close and epic fight at UFC 125.

FORREST GRIFFIN VS. QUINTON JACKSON

Widely considered the greatest fight of 2008, Griffin's leg kicks were the difference at UFC 86, July 5, in Las Vegas.

Forrest Griffin wasn't supposed to get this far. That was the prevailing opinion as the original *Ultimate Fighter* winner challenged Quinton "Rampage" Jackson for the UFC lightweight championship in the main event of UFC 86 at the Mandalay Bay, Las Vegas.

Griffin had been on the verge of quitting mixed martial arts before he was accepted as a cast member on a new UFC reality show called *The Ultimate Fighter.* Although he had won the whole series—culminating in that unforgettable war with Stephan Bonnar in the finale—getting outpointed by veteran Tito Ortiz and a first-round KO loss to Keith Jardine suggested the Las Vegas native was an exciting contender, sure, but perhaps not a world champion in the making.

But when UFC matchmaker Joe Silva struggled to find any willing opponents for new signing Shogun Rua, Griffin seized the chance to catapult himself into the top contenders spot by—to the utter astonishment of most experts—beating up and submitting Rua in three rounds.

The victory earned Griffin a title shot against Rampage, who had dramatically underlined his claim to be the world's greatest 205lb fighter the previous September, beating Dan Henderson over five rounds in London to become the first unified UFC and PRIDE FC champion.

In the opening round, Jackson turned his terrifying power on Griffin. A left hook clipped the challenger high on the head, but it was enough to buckle his legs and, moments later, a left hook/right uppercut combo dropped Griffin hard. But, like he has throughout his career, Griffin refused to wilt and in the second began deploying a genius strategy of attacking Rampage's static legs.

It was an absolute knife-fight for five rounds. Griffin was badly rocked several more times, and Rampage even powerbombed his way out of a triangle attempt. But, while some contest the official unanimous Griffin verdict to this day, Rampage himself was man enough to admit after 25 minutes: "I got my butt kicked!"

Battered, exhausted but now, against all odds, the champion of arguably the UFC's most talented division, Griffin repeated what had become his mantra: "I'm not the best, but I am a guy who will fight the best. And I'll fight them like a dog."

Things are about to get painful for Forrest Griffin as Quinton Jackson prepares to slam him to the mat.

Challenger Griffin fires off a kick at the champion, "Rampage" Jackson.

MICHAEL BISPING VS. YOSHIHIRO AKIYAMA

Rocked by the first punch of the fight, Bisping roared back at UFC 120 at London's O2 Arena, October 16, 2010.

By the time Manchester middleweight Michael Bisping stormed toward the Octagon at approximately 10:20 PM, local time, what the 17,133 Brits who jam-packed the O2 Arena had expected to be a gala evening was already something of a nightmare.

No fewer than five British fighters—James McSweeney, Curt Warburton, James Wilks, John Hathaway, and, most heartbreaking of all for the local fans, Dan Hardy—had gone down in defeat and now all hopes of salvaging British pride from UFC 120 lay with Manchester's Michael Bisping.

The first non-American to ever win *The Ultimate Fighter* and standard-bearer of British MMA since the middle of the decade, "The Count" always carried the expectation of an entire nation with him into the Octagon. But, after watching his friend Hardy get knocked out in a single round by Carlos Condit just 20 minutes prior, Bisping knew the British fans needed him to overcome Japanese icon Yoshihiro Akiyama.

Bisping and Akiyama engage in one of their many UFC 120 exchanges.

The Brits must have feared the worst when a massive Akiyama right hook slammed into Bisping's skull in the opening seconds of the fight. Clearly stunned by the blow, Bisping would later admit he was "completely at sea" for the rest of the round. However, by now a vastly experienced operator, the Englishman also knew that he simply had to fight fire with fire against the Japanese warrior who had earned his reputation as a thunderous puncher.

As the fog gradually lifted, Bisping began to land his left jab regularly on the advancing "Sexyama" and, by round two, was also mixing in takedowns, an arsenal of kicks, and even a flying knee. One of the UFC's most well-tuned cardio machines, Bisping took complete control of the bout in the third, and began lighting up the Osaka native.

In fact, the Brit seemed on the verge of becoming only the second man to ever stop the increasingly exhausted Akiyama when he mistakenly kicked the part-time Japanese model low. When the fight was rejoined, the pair traded once more on equal terms, but Bisping's greater variety of strikes and near-superhuman stamina had earned his 20th career victory and third UFC Fight of the Night.

Akiyama, meanwhile, was noble in defeat and further enhanced his reputation as a magnificent fighting machine, earning his third straight UFC Fight of the Night.

"When I fight in England, the crowd really does get behind me and I feel it's always had a positive impact."
Michael Bisping

TALKING POINT:
BEHIND THE SCENES
ON FIGHT NIGHT

What UFC fans see on the night of an event is the culmination of weeks of hard work by the UFC staff and fighters to make sure that you get the best sporting experience possible.

"Time to roll, baby!" It's the voice and the phrase UFC fighters have come to know so well. Burt Watson, the UFC's longtime site coordinator, is the man with the most important job on fight night other than fighting—he's responsible for getting each athlete out of his locker room, through the arena, and into the Octagon. And considering that there has never been a missing fighter in the history of the UFC, it's clear why Watson is considered the best in the business.

But before he calls each fighter to battle, there is a day-long process needed to produce the most compelling sporting experience in the world. In fact, most aspects of putting together a UFC event begin days, and sometimes weeks, in advance. Whether it's television production, the creation of pre-fight features, public relations, or marketing, the Zuffa machine is always rolling and trying to top each previous show.

Things really kick into gear once the team gets on-site though, and after public relations functions such as open media workouts and the pre-fight press conference finish, it's weigh-in time on the day before the bout. Then, after the fans leave the venue, the crew comes in to build the Octagon, which is the proving ground for mixed martial artists around the world.

On fight day, you can consider the life of a UFC employee to be something like controlled chaos, as everyone scrambles to get multiple jobs done. Here, there is really no such thing as having just one task; if you're working on fight day, odds are you're chipping in wherever needed to make sure things run smoothly.

Early in the day, lighting, television, and sound teams test out the night's music, video features, and lighting routines, and members of the production crew become the main event fighters for a few minutes as they practice the night's Octagon walk-ins. The PR team prepares the media room for the crush of press that will be arriving for the event, and the rest of the team takes care of last-minute ticket requests, credentials, and any other pressing needs.

A few hours before the opening bout, Watson and his team rev up the vans and start bringing the preliminary fighters to the venue. Waiting for them will be some of the world's best cornermen, guys like Jacob "Stitch" Duran and Don House, Rudy Hernandez. This group is available to wrap the hands of the fighters and prepare them for battle, and once the fight starts, they're around to serve as cutmen. It can be the most important job in the corner for a fighter who suffers a cut.

Said Duran: "We get to see these guys at their most vulnerable. We get to see them when we're wrapping their hands, and we get to literally see their heart and soul coming to us, because I always make eye contact with them. We get to see the cuts that they go through, the pain that they go through, and just like any father or mother, we're there to make it as comfortable for them as possible."

Arianny Celeste lets fans know what round it is.

For the veteran fighters of the organization, all of this becomes second nature, as the hustle and bustle in the locker rooms is business as usual. For newcomers though, the first time can be a startling experience. Before taking on Octagon newcomer Ricardo Romero in 2010, veteran light heavyweight Seth Petruzelli said: "I know that he's wrestled for a D-1 school, so I know he's used to wrestling in front of crowds and that sort of thing, so that aspect may not affect him, but definitely the craziness of the UFC and the media and hearing [site coordinator] Burt [Watson]'s voice in the back of the locker room screaming 'It's time baby, it's time.' [Laughs] That might get in his head a little bit, so it's definitely an advantage on my side."

Suddenly, the hours and hours of waiting speed up and feel like seconds. The adrenaline starts flowing, the blood starts pumping and fighters begin pacing in their locker rooms, just waiting to hear Watson. Now, every fighter is the same, even superstars like BJ Penn, who remembers the moments before his UFC 123 bout against Matt Hughes. "I was pumped up and I started screaming 'Call me, call my name. Come on, Burt, call my name.' Even people in the locker room were getting scared.

"Time to roll, baby!"

It's showtime.

The Octagon—mixed martial arts' ultimate proving ground.

"Ninja" Rua gives last-minute instructions to his brother Shogun Rua.

FINISHING MOVES

On any given night, any fighter in the UFC can defeat another one with a variety of different techniques. But there are a few moves that strike fear into opponents even before the bell rings.

Cro Cop's Left Head Kick

"Right leg hospital, left leg cemetery." With those ominous words, Croatia's Mirko Cro Cop set the tone for a career in which he became the most feared striker of his era. And what made his name in the sport was his left kick to the head, a thudding harbinger of doom that almost certainly would knock you out on impact if it landed. What was even more impressive was that Cro Cop didn't even need to throw it to gain his opponents' respect. The anticipation alone left foes open for a laser-like left hand or a whipping right kick, both of which produced their share of knockouts as well. And while Cro Cop made his name with his kicks, his most memorable loss—against Gabriel Gonzaga in 2007—also came via a head kick, making it clear that if you live by the sword, you can die by it as well.

Junior dos Santos just gets out of the way of Mirko Cro Cop's lethal left kick.

One of the more ludicrous statements made about mixed martial arts in recent years was that "leg kicks don't win fights." Well, in the case of Brazilian lightweight contender Edson Barboza, they not only win fights for him, but they also often end them. The only man in UFC history to score two knockouts via leg kicks, the Muay Thai phenom and former champion in the art of eight limbs stopped Mike Lullo and Rafaello Oliveira with shots to the leg that displayed a mix of speed, power, and technique that has been nearly impossible to defend. And when you add in Barboza's knockout of Terry Etim that came by way of a kick to the HEAD, opponents have to be aware of his striking prowess everywhere.

Edson Barboza hobbles Rafaello Oliveira at UFC 162.

Chuck Liddell unleashes his right hand on heated rival Tito Ortiz.

Over the course of seven fights 2004 to 2006, Chuck "The Iceman" Liddell cemented his Hall of Fame legacy with a consecutive knockout streak unlike anything anyone had seen before. And the culprit for most of these devastating finishes was a right hand that could "ice" opponents as soon as he connected it to a chin. And Liddell wasn't knocking out any run-of-the-mill opponents, as Tito Ortiz, Randy Couture, Jeremy Horn, Vernon White, and Renato "Babalu" Sobral all tasted the thunder Liddell packed in his right glove. So what was the secret? Maybe it was that Liddell didn't throw his right in a conventional fashion. Instead, he bent his elbow and swung the right down like a club. Throw in some speed and precision, and more often than not, a direct hit turned into a quick, crowd-pleasing knockout victory.

Jose Aldo's Flying Double Knee

Jose Aldo didn't get thrust into a WEC title shot after his debut win over world-renowned Alexandre Nogueira. Instead, the Brazilian bomber was masterly moved, pitted against solid competition that was expected to test him. But in fact that Aldo made them look ordinary. Three consecutive knockouts of Jonathan Brookins, Rolando Perez, and Chris Mickle made him a must-see for WEC fans, but Cub Swanson was going to be the fighter to push Aldo harder than he had been pushed before. However, that didn't happen. Instead, Aldo came out at the opening bell and landed not one flying knee, but two in quick succession, sending Swanson down to the mat grasping his face, which was sliced open by the assault. The fight took all of eight seconds and marked Aldo —the future WEC and UFC featherweight champion—as one dangerous man.

Cub Swanson feels the heat from Jose Aldo's devastating knees.

Mark Coleman's Ground and Pound

When you hear people refer to UFC Hall of Famer Mark Coleman as "The Godfather of Ground and Pound," it's more than just a sign of respect. It's a confirmation that without Coleman's innovative technique that mixed wrestling with devastating striking, the mixed martial arts world would look a lot different than it does today. A former Division I National wrestling champion for Ohio State University, Coleman moved into the world of MMA in 1996 with little knowledge of standup striking or jiu-jitsu. So "The Hammer" used what he knew best —wrestling—and once he got opponents on the mat, his superior strength and positioning would render them unable to move. And if they did move, they were greeted with an array of punches, elbows, and forearms, making it a miserable night for even the toughest of the tough in the Octagon.

Once Mark Coleman gets you to the mat, it's going to be a long night. Just ask Stephan Bonnar.

Rousimar Palhares' Leg Locks

If Rousimar Palhares gets your leg, the sooner you tap out, the better.

"Panic" is a dirty word in mixed martial arts, and one no fighter wants to have attached to his name in the Octagon. But whenever you see Brazil's Rousimar Palhares grab onto an opponent's foot or leg, the only apt description of the reaction is panic. And that's really no surprise or anything to be ashamed of, as "Toquinho" has a well-deserved reputation for his leg locks, and as nice as the Jiu-Jitsu black belt is outside of competition, when the bell rings and he catches you, he's playing for keeps. Since turning pro in 2006, the majority of his wins have come via some form of leg lock, with UFC opponents Dave Branch, Tomasz Drwal, Lucio Linhares, and Mike Massenzio all being forced to tap out to one of mixed martial arts' most painful submissions practiced by a true master.

Cody McKenzie's Guillotine Choke

Twelve of Cody McKenzie's 14 mixed martial arts wins have come via submission. That's impressive enough. Eleven of those victories were secured with a modified guillotine choke *The Ultimate Fighter* season 12 veteran has dubbed the McKenzietine. Despite being fairly new on the UFC scene, it's as impressive a maneuver as you'll see in the modern fight game, and he's not shy when it comes to talking about its effectiveness. "Yeah, it's that good a move," he says matter-of-factly. "I've caught almost everybody in the world who I rolled with. There's probably only 10 guys who I haven't and I can name them all. [Laughs] And a lot of those 10 guys that just means that they haven't rolled with me enough. If they trained with me a little more or sparred me MMA style, that's when I think I can catch it best."

Cody McKenzie locks up Aaron Wilkinson. A tap is coming up.

Joe Stevenson's Guillotine Choke

A black belt in Brazilian Jiu-Jitsu under the renowned Robert Drysdale, *The Ultimate Fighter* season two winner Joe Stevenson does a lot of things well in the Octagon, but the one thing that has become his Octagon trademark is a guillotine choke that is almost impossible to escape once he slaps it on you. "It's kinda like that bully headlock," said Stevenson, a longtime lightweight contender and former world title challenger who will now be testing his skills in the UFC's new featherweight division. "I lock on to that bad boy and I've got it, so I'm pretty happy with it." Winner of 15 bouts by submission over a career that began in 1999, when he was just 16 years old, "Joe Daddy" has used the guillotine to finish off five opponents, including Dokonjonosuke Mishima, Melvin Guillard, and fellow black belt Gleison Tibau in the UFC.

Anthony Pettis' Showtime Kick

You know a move is special when even the recipient of it can appreciate it, and that was the case with Anthony Pettis' "Showtime" kick at WEC 53 in December of 2010, which wowed the mixed martial arts world and the man who took the shot, then-lightweight champion Ben Henderson. "As a fan, I'm far enough away now that I can admit that kick was amazing," said Henderson. "If I'd have been watching it, I would have been like 'Oh my God, that was awesome.' Sadly, I was the one being kicked in the head." So what was so special about it? How about everything, as Pettis took a leap off the fence, and with the right leg he used to propel himself toward Henderson he kicked his foe, knocking him down and sending everyone into a shock that they'll never forget.

Anthony Pettis is one of the most creative offensive fighters in the sport today.

Anderson Silva's Front Kick

When you talk about the arsenal of UFC middleweight champion Anderson Silva, you can spend hours breaking down the various moves that "The Spider" uses to dismantle and defeat his opponents. But in the interest of saving space and giving some other fighters their time to shine, we'll narrow it down to one of his most recent signature finishing moves, a blistering front kick that took everyone by surprise—especially opponent Vitor Belfort—when he revealed it in the first round of the UFC 126 main event in February of 2011. Fired off with speed and precision, Silva nailed Belfort flush on the jaw with the kick, and "The Phenom" fell as if he had been shot. The finishing punches were just window-dressing as it was the kick—which Silva said was taught to him by action film star Steven Seagal—that truly did the job.

Pound-for-pound king Anderson Silva unleashes devastating front kick to Vitor Belfont's jaw in the first round of their UFC 126 encounter.

12

Number of post fight bonus awards won by —**Anderson Silva**

6

Number of UFC champions faced by **Stephan Bonnar**— Anderson Silva, Lyoto Machida, Forrest Griffin, Rashad Evans, Jon Jones, Mark Coleman

THE *UFC* IN NUMBERS

It's been said that a picture says a thousand words. In mixed martial arts, some statistics speak louder about a fighter's accomplishments than a well timed left hook. So here are some key UFC numbers.

Number of UFC world titles won by **Randy Couture**

11-0

Georges St-Pierre's record in fights that go the distance

3

Number of The Ultimate Fighter season winners to win a UFC title —**Forrest Griffin, Matt Serra, Rashad Evans**

UFC

1

Number of fights ended by the "Twister" submission—*Chan Sung Jung over Leonard Garcia*

84.5

inches – *Jones'* reach, which is tied with seven foot heavyweight Stefan Struve for the longest in UFC history

16

Number of fighters to have won all three post-fight awards – KO, Sub, and Fight of the Night— *Chan Sung Jung, Stefan Struve, Jon Jones, Ed Herman, BJ Penn, Georges St-Pierre, Anderson Silva, Dennis Siver, Josh Koscheck, Chris Lytle, Paulo Thiago, Marcus Davis, Wilson Gouveia, Donald Cerrone, Joe Lauzon, Tito Ortiz*

23

years old – Age of the youngest title holder in UFC history, *Jon Jones*, when he won the belt

9

Number of Brazilian fighters to win a UFC title —*Anderson Silva, Junior dos Santos, Vitor Belfort, Mauricio Rua, Murilo Bustamante, Jose Aldo, Antonio Rodrigo Nogueira, Renan Barao, Lyoto Machida*

PHILIPPIANS 4:13

OCTAGON GIRL:

BRITTNEY PALMER

Las Vegas' Brittney Palmer first came to mixed martial arts after a stint as a boxing ring card girl, and once she got her first dose of MMA action as part of the WEC organization, she was hooked.

"There's really no comparison," said Ms. Palmer. "When you're watching boxing, it's like 'okay, they can throw punches,' but when you're watching MMA, it's just so much better. When you're happy to be there and happy to watch it, you're happy to be working.

And nothing makes the brunette bombshell happier than working a big room, like she has in arenas around the world with the WEC, and then, the UFC.

"The more people the better – go big or go home," laughs Brittney, who is a talented artist and popular ambassador for the sport when she's not working Octagonside on fight night. "It's such an adrenaline rush. And even though we're just the ring card girls, it's really cool to be part of something that big."

Popular UFC Ring girl Brittney Palmer is an aspiring artist, a model and a television host.

COMEBACKS OF ALL TIME

While dominating knockout and submission victories are exciting in their own right, there's something about a come from behind win that belongs in a category all of its own. Here are 10 such memorable comebacks.

Anderson Silva Wsub5 Chael Sonnen

UFC 117 The drama before this UFC 117 bout took place in August of 2010 couldn't hold a candle to what happened on fight night, as Anderson Silva and Chael Sonnen engaged in a middleweight title bout for the ages. Yes, Sonnen dominated the majority of the bout with his ground and pound attack, but each moment before he would take the previously untouchable titleholder to the mat was filled with tension as Silva unleashed the strikes many believed would end the fight. But even though he got rocked on a few occasions, Sonnen was resolute in his attack, and as the seconds ticked by, he was getting closer and closer to one of the sport's great upsets and the realization of a dream. But then, like the truest of true champions, Silva pulled off a fifth-round submission win, and calling it a spectacular comeback simply doesn't do it justice.

Things aren't looking too good for Anderson Silva here against Chael Sonnen, but "The Spider" would bounce back soon enough.

Roger Huerta vs. Clay Guida

TUF 6 To be considered great, a fight has to have more than frantic action and back and forth momentum swings, though those attributes certainly don't hurt. What a fight truly needs to enter the realm of the classics is drama, and the December 2007 bout between Roger Huerta and Clay Guida on *The Ultimate Fighter 6* Finale card lived up to that end of the bargain spectacularly. Down two rounds to none on all three judges' scorecards, Huerta needed to stop or submit Guida in the final round to win. These two trains met in the center of the Octagon in round three and collided, with Huerta's knee knocking Guida off track. "The Carpenter" gamely and frantically tried to recover, but Huerta wouldn't allow it, and "El Matador" eventually got Guida's back and sunk in a fight-ending rear naked choke 51 seconds into the third stanza.

Roger Huerta's fighting heart kept him in his match with Clay Guida until he could turn things around.

Mike Russow KO3 Todd Duffee

One punch is all it took for Mike Russow to erase Todd Duffee's lead on the scorecards and take the victory.

UFC 114 For 12 minutes and 30 seconds, highly touted heavyweight prospect Todd Duffee was sailing to his second UFC win in as many tries. He came out fast against Mike Russow at UFC 114 in May of 2010, and he rocked and dropped his opponent in the early going. To Russow's credit, he shook off the blows and stood in there, hoping for the opening he needed to get the fight to the mat, but that opening never showed up, and Duffee's striking prowess allowed him to win the first and second rounds big. Nothing changed in round three, with Duffee still dominating, but suddenly Russow drilled Duffee on the chin with a right hand over the top that started to send him toward the canvas. A follow-up right finished the job at the 2:35 mark, and just like that, Mike Russow was victorious.

Chris Leben Wsub3 Yoshihiro Akiyama

UFC 116 It wasn't an enviable position for Chris Leben to be in. *The Ultimate Fighter* season 1 standout was coming off a stirring knockout victory over Aaron Simpson, yet just two weeks later he was standing in the Octagon in Las Vegas again, as a late replacement against Japanese superstar Yoshihiro Akiyama at UFC 116 in July 2010. For two rounds, it was a back-and-forth scrap, with each middleweight taking turns teeing off on the other. Defense was purely optional at this point, but as the third round commenced, the rigors of fighting twice in two weeks began to wear on Leben, and Akiyama turned up the heat. Akiyama put his foe on the mat and began to deliver what he believed to be the finishing ground strikes, but out of nowhere, Leben slapped on a tight triangle choke and Akiyama tapped out with just 20 seconds left. Simply amazing.

Chris Leben and Yoshihiro Akiyama scrap in one of the best fights of 2010.

Carlos Condit TKO3 Rory MacDonald

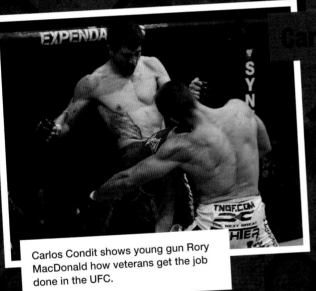

Carlos Condit shows young gun Rory MacDonald how veterans get the job done in the UFC.

UFC 115 Going into their UFC 115 match in June of 2010, fight fans wondered whether 20-year-old wunderkind Rory "The Waterboy" MacDonald had the experience to hang with "The Natural Born Killer," former WEC welterweight champion Carlos Condit. Well, that answer came early and often, as MacDonald took the first two rounds of the bout thanks to a dynamic attack that kept the aggressive Condit off balance at every turn. In the process, MacDonald's home country fans in Vancouver, Canada, got louder and louder as they cheered their hero on. But in the third, Condit's experience paid off as he got MacDonald to the mat and ground and pounded his way to a stirring TKO victory with only seven seconds left in the bout. In the end, Condit got the victory, MacDonald got respect, and the fans got a fight they would never forget.

Scott Smith KO2 Pete Sell

Scott Smith and Pete Sell leave defense at the door in their middleweight brawl.

TUF 4 Unless it's a sudden one-punch or one-kick knockout, you can usually see when a finish is coming in MMA. But never was there such a swing in emotions as when Pete Sell fought Scott Smith at *The Ultimate Fighter 4* Finale in November of 2006. It was the second round of what had been an action-packed standup battle, and the two buddies continued to throw caution to the wind. And while it looked like Smith was pulling into the lead, Sell fired back with a shot to the body that hurt Smith and sent him reeling backward. The end was probably a punch or two away, and Sell knew it. But in his haste to finish, he got careless, and Smith—who admitted he had only one punch left in him—swung for the fences and landed, ending Sell's night at 3:25 of the second round.

France's Cheick Kongo rescues victory from the jaws of defeat against Pat Barry.

UFC LIVE Given all the disappointments seen when bouts pitting striker against striker instead turned into a wrestling match, expectations were that Cheick Kongo would take Pat Barry down in their June 2011 bout or that "HD" would even attempt to show off his own growing ground game against the Frenchman. But thankfully, the two decided to live up to their striking reputations, and what followed was a tense trading of thudding leg kicks until all hell broke loose when Barry sent Kongo to the canvas twice, both times appearing to be seconds away from a stoppage victory. But just when all seemed to be lost for Kongo, he got to his feet, planted them, and then ripped off two right hands. The first one stunned Barry, the second put him on his back, and when referee Dan Miragliotta halted the bout, Kongo had just delivered the most spectacular comeback win since Scott Smith finished Pete Sell in 2006.

UFC 75 After 20 professional boxing matches in which his only loss came via cuts, Marcus "The Irish Hand Grenade" Davis had proved the sturdiness of his chin in the most trying of situations. It remained undented in his mixed martial arts career as well, and heading into his UFC 75 match against England's "Relentless" Paul Taylor in September of 2007, Davis sported a nine-fight winning streak and a boatload of confidence. Yet Taylor, who kept the pressure on for much of the opening frame, put that streak in jeopardy when he dropped Davis for the first time with a thudding kick to the neck. It looked like lights out for the American, but suddenly, the former pro-boxer turned the tide, and he didn't do it with a haymaker, he did it with an armbar, continuing his evolution as an MMA fighter in his most impressive win to date.

Paul Taylor stunned Marcus Davis early, but it was "The Irish Hand Grenade" who got the last word and the win.

Rocked, but never out, Chris Leben showed his resilience in knocking out Terry Martin.

UFC FN11 After losing three of his previous four fights, Chris Leben needed a win in the worst way when he took on hard-hitting Terry Martin on a UFC Fight Night card in September of 2007. And he was impressive early on as he mixed up his attack with knees, kicks, punches, and foot stomps, keeping Martin from getting into a steady rhythm. But what was apparently a Leben round went for naught when a slam by Martin was nullified by a fence grab that cost "The Crippler" a point. The second was better for Leben scorecard-wise, but in the third, Martin roared back, hitting the mark with a right hand that shook Leben. Another right followed, yet just when the end seemed near, Leben came back with a left hook on the jaw that laid Martin out and forced a stoppage by referee Herb Dean at 3:56 of the final round.

In a career of great performances, Matt Hughes' rematch win over Frank Trigg may have been the greatest.

Matt Hughes Wsub1 Frank Trigg

UFC 52 Despite losing to Matt Hughes in their first bout, Frank Trigg was not about to concede that the welterweight champion was the better fighter. So when he got a second shot at UFC 52 in April of 2005, he was determined to turn the tables. Early on, Trigg caught Hughes with a low knee that was not caught by referee Mario Yamasaki. As Hughes retreated, Trigg pounced and sent Hughes to the canvas with a left to the jaw and followed up with a rear naked choke attempt. Hughes' face turned crimson, but amazingly he was able to escape and then follow up this good fortune by picking his foe up and carrying him across the cage before dropping him with a trademark slam. Now it was Hughes in control as he sunk in his own rear naked choke, which produced a tap out at the 4:05 mark.

UFC

TALKING POINT

FIGHT STRATEGY AND
MENTAL ATTITUDE

A fighter enters the Octagon alone, barefoot, and stripped to the waist. Staring back at him is another highly skilled, dangerous athlete with very bad intentions... mental strength is not optional in the UFC.

For even the bravest among us, the idea of sitting backstage in a huge, packed arena waiting to have a professional fight is a scary one.

The mantra of "positive mental attitude" is something all of us remember from high-school sports, but perhaps in no other sport are self-belief and courage as important as they are in the UFC.

As UFC President Dana White put it: "This isn't the place to find out if you are a tough guy or not. You better know you are a tough guy before you get here because you will be found out pretty quick. What these guys do isn't easy, most of us can't do it. Some people say guys like Tito Ortiz, Michael Bisping, or Josh Koscheck are arrogant but, guess what? These guys are fighters. They have to be that way to even step in there and attempt to do what they do. You better believe in yourself, because if you don't the Octagon isn't the place for you."

That's not to suggest that UFC fighters don't experience doubts, performance anxiety, and even fear though. Some of the best fighters in the world will readily admit they experience fear when they go to work, and conquering that fear is vital if they are to have any chance of success when the time comes to perform.

Welterweight Dan "The Outlaw" Hardy has operated at the elite level of competition for over three years. He is best known for his brash confidence and refusing to submit despite getting dominated by Georges St-Pierre at UFC 111. A thoughtful, well-read individual outside the Octagon, Hardy says every fighter must overcome fear and doubt each time he enters the arena of battle.

He said, "There's an anxiety and nervousness. I'm a confident person, but I get butterflies as I leave the dressing room and walk to the tunnel leading to the arena. That's when the real nerves hit. I think 'I have to perform right now—this is it!'

"But once I am into the arena, they go away. I don't know if it is the cheers or what, but by the time I reach the Octagon, they are gone entirely. All the buzz, the energy is there, but it has changed from nervous, negative energy to positive, confident energy."

UFC lightweight champion Frankie Edgar also experiences what he calls "an anxiety build" as the fight draws near. He said a professional learns to lessen the impact nerves have on their fight performance as he moves through his career.

Dan "The Outlaw" Hardy entering the arena at UFC Fight Night 24.

Thiago Silva gets some key advice from his trainer between rounds.

"The Answer" explained: "At the start of my career I would get the call the fight was on and—boom—I'd have a knot in my stomach which wouldn't go away until after the fight. Fight night, obviously, it would be the worst. But as I went on in my career I've managed to control the nerves and even use them to help me."

He added: "You learn to concentrate on the positives and not let negative stuff play on your mind. For example, I learned to believe being smaller has advantages. Like against BJ Penn I was able to use my lower center of gravity and head movement to avoid his boxing and also score a couple of takedowns. I used to look at bigger opponents and think about them being stronger, but experience has taught me that's not usually the case."

It is one thing to feel confident when in the flush of good health but, as UFC middleweight champion Michael Bisping reveals, very few fighters make it through an eight-week training camp without picking up a sprain, twinge, or cold.

"You never fight at 100 percent," "The Count" said. "You've always got a bump or bruise, a banged up elbow, or a stubbed toe. You get injured far more in training than you do in the Octagon, but you have to deal with it. Plus, all that training, pushing your body, lowers your immune system and you are forever picking up colds and man-flus, it could be tempting to think 'Poor me, I'm not at my best so why not fight another day,' but, for me, pulling out of a fight is not an option. I am a fighter and my job is to suck it up. It is important to realize, mentally, that your opponent won't be 100 percent either. You have to believe that you've put in the work and you will win no matter what. You have to have that self-belief."

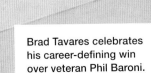

Brad Tavares celebrates his career-defining win over veteran Phil Baroni.

HALL OF FAME

Fighters have come and gone over the years, and all have made a contribution to UFC history. But only a select few have earned induction to the UFC Hall of Fame.

UFC Hall of Famer Chuck "The Iceman" Liddell celebrates a victory as only he can.

You can never forget November 12, 1993. On that night in Denver, a sport was born in the United States and there's just one man to thank—Royce Gracie.

Sure, you have to consider Rorion Gracie, Royce's brother, for starting the event, as well as all the businessmen working behind the scenes and the other fighters that competed at McNichols Arena that fall evening, but let's not mince words—if the first Ultimate Fighting Championship was won by a ripped monster with otherworldly athletic skills, the event (and the sport) probably would have faded away.

Face it, people tuned in to the first UFC to see blood. Instead, they saw the underdog of underdogs enter the Octagon and beat everyone who was supposed to annihilate him. In just under five minutes, he scored three victories and the name "Gracie" became a household word. That night, mixed martial arts started on the road it is still traveling today, where it is no longer a spectacle but a sport; where you can turn on your television and see free fight cards, or buy DVDs of the latest pay-per-view event and a UFC t-shirt.

Needless to say, to have that much on your shoulders is the type of pressure that could break lesser men. But as the standard-bearer for Gracie jiu-jitsu, the Rio de Janeiro native had the confidence to step into competition and the skills to succeed.

That night marked the beginning of the Gracie legend, and in a world where that word is over- and improperly used, Royce Gracie is the real deal. But with the grace that has become his trademark, ask him about this and he deflects the praise from himself effortlessly.

"The legend is my father," said Royce of the renowned Hélio Gracie. "He's the man who created this whole no-holds-barred deal, who came up with the concepts. I'm just a fighter; I'm just doing my job."

That's always been the appeal of Gracie. He would come into the arena surrounded by family, do his thing once the bell rang, and then would leave the same way he came in. No trash talk, no posturing, no "me, me, me," just an athlete, like he said, doing his job.

And from 1993 to 1995, Gracie did his job better than anyone else in the growing sport, compiling an 11-0-1, 1 NC record, with the only blemishes being a draw with Ken Shamrock and a no contest against Harold Howard at UFC 3, when he was forced to withdraw due to exhaustion from a grueling bout earlier that 1994 night with Kimo Leopoldo. So, in effect, Gracie never lost in his early years of UFC competition, a streak that was only broken in 2006 when he returned to the Octagon at 39 and was stopped by Matt Hughes.

But that defeat would never tarnish the legacy of the UFC's first warrior, Royce Gracie, the man who paved the way for all the fighters who followed him.

PROFILE

WEIGHT CLASS: Welterweight
DATE OF BIRTH: December 12, 1966
HEIGHT/WEIGHT: 6ft 1in, 176lb
BIRTHPLACE: Rio de Janeiro, Brazil
FIGHTING OUT OF: Torrance, CA
STYLE: Gracie jiu-jitsu
PROFESSIONAL MMA RECORD: 14-2-3, 1 No Contest

Royce Gracie looks to recapture glory in his 2006 bout with Matt Hughes.

Ken Shamrock waits for the bell to ring to wade into battle once again.

KEN SHAMROCK

Known as "The World's Most Dangerous Man," Ken Shamrock will be best remembered by UFC fans for his memorable rivalries with Royce Gracie and Tito Ortiz, bouts that captivated the mixed martial arts world.

"Honor is not about winning—honor is about you stepping up and standing for what you believe in, and that's it," said Shamrock. "That's what I do—if somebody says something to me or does something to me, I will stand up."

That's not to say that the Georgia native—who was inducted into the UFC Hall of Fame in 2003—didn't have his share of big wins, as he defeated Dan Severn, Kimo Leopoldo (twice), Brian Johnston, and Patrick Smith over the course of a UFC career that also saw him coach against Ortiz in season three of *The Ultimate Fighter*. But it may have been the three-fight series against Ortiz that truly captured the world's imagination.

"He's an emotional fighter, I'm an emotional fighter, and anything that goes on, we tend to amplify it, just because that's what gets us going," he said. "All the things that you see happening between me and Tito, it was real, there's no question about that. But we amplify it."

What many may not know though is that Shamrock's career started in Japan, where he became the first ever King of Pancrase, one of the sport's most prestigious titles. Even while he became a UFC pioneer, he would shuttle to Japan for Pancrase fights, compiling a 17-4 record in the organization. Yet despite his success there and with PRIDE, Shamrock was remembered most for his stint in the UFC, and even his fiercest rival, Ortiz, gave him his respect after their third and final fight in 2006.

"People see the intensity that he brought in," said Ortiz. "When he came in, people looked at him like 'Wow, this guy is one of the world's most dangerous men' and he brought a lot to the game and carried it all the way up until I got into it."

Shamrock would have his wins and losses in the game, but when it came down to it, few fighters captivated the public the way he did and perhaps no one could get fans interested in a fight quite like he did.

"It's the feuds," he said with a smile. "That's something that really drove me and something that I'm sure the fans really got into. You go all the way back to the first UFC, and the first feud was me and Royce Gracie, then it was Dan Severn and myself—we had a little spat at a press conference—then Kimo, and then it's been me and Tito ever since."

The way Shamrock saw it, love him or hate him, you were going to watch him, and in the end, it's all about putting people in the seats and giving them a great fight. In those respects, Ken Shamrock always scored a knockout.

PROFILE

WEIGHT CLASS: Light heavyweight / heavyweight
DATE OF BIRTH: February 11, 1964
HEIGHT/WEIGHT: 6ft, 205lb
BIRTHPLACE: Macon, GA
FIGHTING OUT OF: Susanville, CA
STYLE: Submission fighting
PROFESSIONAL MMA RECORD: 28-15-2

DAN SEVERN — "THE BEAST"

Dan Severn, the first world-class wrestler to compete in the Ultimate Fighting Championship and a winner of two tournaments and two superfights, became the third member of the UFC Hall of Fame at UFC 52 in 2005.

"Dan Severn showed the world that wrestling was a formidable fighting art and he opened the door for other top wrestlers to enter the UFC and be successful," said UFC President Dana White.

Severn made an immediate impression at UFC 4 in December of 1994, as he defeated Anthony Macias and Marcus Bossett in devastating fashion, setting up a tournament final bout against the sport's first superstar, the seemingly unbeatable jiu-jitsu master Royce Gracie.

But considering Severn's wrestling pedigree as a two-time All-American for Arizona State University and a competitor in the 1984 and 1988 Olympic trials, those in the know realised that he was the only person capable of giving Gracie a fight. And what a fight he gave, as he dominated the action for over 15 minutes until Gracie pulled victory from the jaws of defeat and finally locked in a finishing triangle choke to win his third Ultimate Fighting Championship.

Severn's journey in the Octagon was just beginning though, as he compiled a 7-3 UFC record, beating the likes of Oleg Taktarov, Dave Beneteau, Ken Shamrock, and Tank Abbott along the way. Perhaps even more importantly, he paved the way for his fellow wrestlers to enter and become successful in mixed martial arts. Today, it's no surprise that the dominant combat discipline in the UFC is wrestling, and it was fighters like "The Beast" who were pioneers. And let's not forget that the world-renowned fighter helped launch both PRIDE and the WEC by appearing in their inaugural shows in 1997 and 2001 respectively.

In September of 2000, Severn competed in his final UFC bout, losing to Pedro Rizzo at UFC 27, but years later, the Michigan native was still competing at the age of 54. That's an amazing feat, and further proof that Severn – who fought the likes of Forrest Griffin, Wes Sims, Justin Eilers, Dan Christison, Seth Petruzelli and Colin Robinson in non-UFC bouts – was one of a kind.

PROFILE

WEIGHT CLASS: Heavyweight
DATE OF BIRTH: June 8, 1958
HEIGHT/WEIGHT: 6ft 2in, 250lb
BIRTHPLACE: Coldwater, MI
FIGHTING OUT OF: Coldwater, MI
STYLE: Wrestling
PROFESSIONAL MMA RECORD: 101-19-7

A dominant force in the early days of the UFC, Dan Severn holds up the spoils of victory.

Randy Couture's contribution to the UFC has been immense.

RANDY COUTURE — "THE NATURAL"

Usually, you have to wait a number of years before getting the opportunity to be honored as a member of a sport's Hall of Fame, whether it be football, baseball, or boxing.

But when Randy Couture retired after a February 2006 defeat to Chuck Liddell, the wait wasn't years, but a mere four months, as "The Natural" was inducted into the UFC Hall of Fame during the finale of *The Ultimate Fighter 3*. And if anyone in the sport deserved a speedy entry into the Hall, it was Couture.

"It's nice to be honored and to be recognized with guys like Royce [Gracie] and Ken [Shamrock] and Dan Severn," said the Washington state native. "They were all guys that I looked up to and admired when they started fighting, and I said, 'Man, I've really got to try that.'"

He not only tried it, he became a legend at it. A decorated wrestler who was a three-time US Olympic alternate and All-American for Oklahoma State University, Couture turned his sights to mixed martial arts and made his debut at UFC 13 on May 30, 1997 with wins over Tony Halme and Stephen Graham.

It was less than five months later that Couture really made an impact on the scene as he stopped the seemingly unbeatable Vitor Belfort at UFC 15 and followed that up in December of 1997 with a decision win over Maurice Smith that earned him the first of multiple UFC titles.

A contract dispute took him out of the UFC for close to three years, but when he returned to the organization in 2000, he picked up right where he left off, stopping Kevin Randleman in three rounds to win the heavyweight crown a second time.

Two successful title defenses followed before he lost back-to-back bouts to the much bigger Josh Barnett and Ricco Rodriguez. Seemingly done at the age of 39, Couture made a drop down to the light heavyweight division, where most questioned whether he could compete with the young superstars at 205lb.

Well, compete he did, beating Chuck Liddell, Tito Ortiz, and Vitor Belfort (a fluke injury-induced loss to Belfort being the only blemish on his record during his 2003–04 campaigns) and establishing himself as a true MMA great.

Couture would lose two of his next three bouts, both to Liddell, but then, amazingly, the newly minted Hall of Famer would return from his 2006 retirement a year later to defeat 6ft 8in giant Tim Sylvia at UFC 68 to win the heavyweight championship an unprecedented third time.

That would have been enough to further cement his legacy, but Couture continued to compete against the likes of Brock Lesnar, Gabriel Gonzaga, and Antonio Rodrigo Nogueira until a career ending loss to Lyoto Machida at UFC 129 in 2011.

PROFILE

WEIGHT CLASS: Light heavyweight / heavyweight
DATE OF BIRTH: June 22, 1963
HEIGHT/WEIGHT: 6ft 2in, 205lb
BIRTHPLACE: Everett, WA
FIGHTING OUT OF: Las Vegas, NV
STYLE: Wrestling
PROFESSIONAL MMA RECORD: 19-10

MARK COLEMAN "THE HAMMER"

The next time you watch a UFC event and see a fighter score a double-leg takedown, proceed to change position effortlessly, and then ground and pound his opponent out, you can rest assured that Mark "The Hammer" Coleman had something to do with it.

"I'd like to think I've had some influence on some guys," he said. "I'm just really glad I could be part of taking the whole sport to the level where it's at right now."

Yet after a stellar amateur wrestling career that saw him win a NCAA Championship in 1988 for Ohio State University, earn All-American status twice, and also compete for the United States in the 1992 Olympic Games, Coleman was 31 and didn't know where his athletic career was going to lead him. But then he turned on the television and saw the Ultimate Fighting Championship.

"The first time I saw it I thought it was the greatest thing I had ever seen in my life," he said. With talent, athleticism, and unbelievable strength, Coleman showed it all in his UFC debut on July 12, 1996, as he romped over Moti Horenstein, Gary Goodridge, and Don Frye in one night to win the UFC 10 tournament and become an instant MMA star.

Just two months later, Coleman was back in the Octagon and he was even more devastating, beating Julian Sanchez and Brian Johnston in a combined 3:05 to win the UFC 11 tournament in Augusta, Georgia, and in February of 1997, he capped off his amazing run with a two-minute, 57-second win over UFC standout (and fellow Hall of Famer) Dan Severn to become the first UFC heavyweight champion.

Coleman's winning streak came to an end at UFC 14 when he was decisioned by Maurice Smith, and while he left the organization after subsequent setbacks at the hands of Pete Williams and Pedro Rizzo, you couldn't keep him down, and after a brief break, he traveled to Japan to compete in the PRIDE organization, where he resurrected his career, won the PRIDE Grand Prix finals in 2000, and reestablished himself as one of the best heavyweights in the world.

But his heart always stayed with the UFC, where he returned in 2009 for three bouts that included a win over Stephan Bonnar and a Fight of the Night war with Shogun Rua that reminded fight fans just who "The Hammer" was.

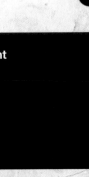

PROFILE

WEIGHT CLASS: Heavyweight / light heavyweight
DATE OF BIRTH: December 20, 1964
HEIGHT/WEIGHT: 6ft 1in, 205lb
BIRTHPLACE: Columbus, OH
FIGHTING OUT OF: Columbus, OH
STYLE: Wrestling
PROFESSIONAL MMA RECORD: 16-10

Credited as the "Godfather of ground and pound," Mark Coleman has been one of the UFC's most ferocious competitors.

Willing to take one to give one, Chuck Liddell sets up another knockout win.

CHUCK LIDDELL — "THE ICEMAN"

Every fight fan knows who Chuck Liddell is. Camera crews follow him around, flocks of reporters jot down his every word, but, remarkably, he has remained the same person he's always been.

Sure, the bank account's bigger, the clubs are nicer, and the trappings of fame more expensive – both literally and figuratively – but of everyone in professional sports today, Liddell has remained truest to what got him here in the first place.

"The Iceman" has the same Mohawk, the same friends, and the same attitude. He has always boiled fighting down to its bare essence. When he stepped into the Octagon, it was a fight—not a chess match, not a clashing of styles or comparison of techniques. He was going to hit you, you were going to try to hit him, and more often than not, you were going to fall down. It was a fight, plain and simple, and no one wanted to win more than he did.

That was bad news for the men he faced in the Octagon. From 2004 to 2007, he went on a tear that established him not only as the game's unquestioned superstar, but as the most terrifying light heavyweight in the game. Strangely enough though, as Liddell's fame grew, the respect he received (and still receives) from his peers never waned. Liddell was a true fighter's fighter, and that's an accolade you can't buy or receive from newspaper clippings or television appearances.

And during his reign of terror over the UFC's 205lb weight class, he wasn't beating cupcakes, as his seven-fight unbeaten streak during that span included wins over world champions Randy Couture (twice) and Tito Ortiz (twice), as well as respected contenders like Babalu Sobral and Jeremy Horn. What made this run even more spectacular was that he won all of those bouts by knockout.

On the day before UFC 100 in July of 2009, Liddell was inducted into the UFC Hall of Fame. It was the type of celebration that he would probably do anything to steer clear of, as he was never about the attention. It was always about the fight, and when asked how he would like to be remembered a hundred years from now, his answer spoke volumes.

"As a fighter," said Liddell. "As someone who didn't duck anyone, someone who fought everybody that came up, and that always came out there to fight tough."

PROFILE

WEIGHT CLASS: Light heavyweight
DATE OF BIRTH: December 17, 1969
HEIGHT/WEIGHT: 6ft 2in, 205lb
BIRTHPLACE: Santa Barbara, CA
FIGHTING OUT OF: San Luis Obispo, CA
STYLE: Kickboxing
PROFESSIONAL MMA RECORD: 21-8

MATT HUGHES

In 2010, Matt Hughes was inducted into the UFC Hall of Fame for achievements which included seven successful title defenses over two reigns as welterweight champion, and stellar victories over a who's who at 170lb.

But back in 2001 he was just another welterweight, 2-1 in the UFC and assuming that he was on his way back to his farm to work full-time.

Then came a stirring second-round knockout victory over Carlos Newton that earned him the UFC welterweight title and began a run that most fighters could only dream of as he went on to defeat Mach Sakurai, Newton in a rematch, Gil Castillo, Sean Sherk, and Frank Trigg.

Hughes would lose his crown at UFC 46 in 2004, but nine months later he was back on top after beating a pretty fair 170lb fighter in his own right in Georges St-Pierre. In Hughes' first defense of his second reign, he was pitted against Trigg again, and what resulted was one of the greatest fights in UFC history.

Yet while the come-from-behind submission win over Trigg could have been enough for Hughes to hang his hat and walk into the sunset, the pride of Hillsboro, Illinois, wasn't done yet. After that win, he defeated Joe Riggs, Royce Gracie, BJ Penn, Chris Lytle, Matt Serra, Ricardo Almeida, and Renzo Gracie, with his only losses coming to St-Pierre (twice), Thiago Alves, and Penn. Along the way he built a diehard fan following that has stuck with him for over a decade, a rarity among rarities these days.

And at 36, Matt Hughes was a Hall of Famer. It was something he still couldn't believe.

"I took this up as just a hobby, something to occupy my time and to vent some aggressiveness and be competitive," he said. "I never thought that I would be in the position that I'm in today. If I want a new car, I can trade my truck in and get a new car. My kids have got shoes and clothes and we don't worry about food on the table. Shaking hands, signing autographs, being a world titleholder and being inducted into the Hall of Fame, this is beyond what I ever would have pictured my life being. I'm supposed to be that guy with a shovel or a hammer in his hands, and he's working hard. That's just who I am."

PROFILE

WEIGHT CLASS: Welterweight
DATE OF BIRTH: October 13, 1973
HEIGHT/WEIGHT: 5ft 9in, 170lb
BIRTHPLACE: Hillsboro, IL
FIGHTING OUT OF: Hillsboro, IL
STYLE: H.I.T. Squad
PROFESSIONAL MMA RECORD: 46-9

Matt Hughes pushes the action against his longtime rival BJ Penn.

The beloved TapouT crew, led by founder Charles "Mask" Lewis.

CHARLES "MASK" LEWIS

Charles "Mask" Lewis was always a staunch supporter of mixed martial arts, even in its darkest days, and one of the select few who can rightly claim to be a pioneer in the sport.

Charles "Mask" Lewis started the TapouT clothing company with Dan Caldwell (aka "Punkass") in 1997, not with a business degree and a marketing plan, but with a true love for a sport that made an impact on him the first time he saw Royce Gracie in 1993.

"I bought every color Gracie jiu-jitsu shirt," said Lewis. "I don't think they made it in pink, but if they had, I would have bought that too. [Laughs] It was like my armor when I went out into the world. I bet I could walk on water and the sea would part with this shirt on."

Soon, Lewis would come up with his own armor—shirts with the logo TapouT on them—and in the process of selling the shirts out of the trunk of his car and at local MMA shows, he helped build a brand that is synonymous with the sport today, one that you can find not only at every fight event, but in your local shopping mall. Needless to say, his perseverance paid off.

Yet strangely enough, despite TapouT's emergence as a multi-million-dollar company, what people may remember Lewis most for is his unmistakable war paint and outfits that forever branded him as "Mask."

"I don't care if you call us the TapouT guys, TapouT crew, TapouT fools, two nerds and a cool guy—you know who we are," he said. "Mask allows me to give my true opinion at all times. Who cares about Clark Kent? I want Superman. You don't care about Bruce Wayne, Bruce Banner, Clark Kent—you want the superhero. I hated *Spider-Man 3* when Tobey Maguire was going around without his gear on. I was like 'Will you put your damn outfit on?'"

Then he would just laugh, and if you ever heard him let it loose, it was infectious. That's how his personality was as well, and if you walked away from a conversation with him without liking him, there was something wrong with you.

Tragically, "Mask" was killed in an automobile crash on March 11, 2009. Yet while the MMA world misses his presence, it will never forget him, and he will forever be immortalized in the UFC Hall of Fame.

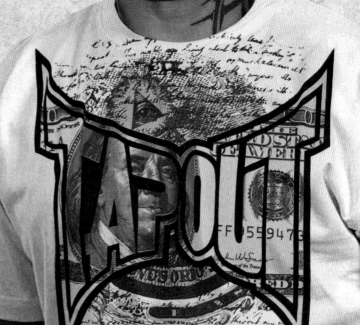

PROFILE

DATE OF BIRTH: June 23, 1963
DIED: March 11, 2009
ACHIEVEMENT: Founder of TapouT

Love him or hate him, Tito Ortiz always drew a reaction from fight fans.

TITO ORTIZ

A longtime light heavyweight champion, Tito Ortiz's slams, ground and pound, and "Bad Boy" persona made him a crossover star in the early years of the Zuffa era, and his memorable battles with Ken Shamrock, Chuck Liddell, Randy Couture, and Forrest Griffin built a legendary legacy that established him as one of the most popular fighters ever and earned him a spot in the UFC Hall of Fame in 2012.

"It's recognition and I'm thankful," he said. "It's always been my goal in life to be the best athlete that I could be and that ever graced the Octagon, and not only inside, but outside. I wanted to be an inspiration in a lot of people's lives, so they could look at this sport and not see it as barbaric human cockfighting, but see us as well-trained athletes that compete against each other to see who the best athlete is. And I've done that, I think. I helped break the mold. I fought in three decades, and it's crazy to even imagine that.

"I gave my heart, soul, and body to this sport and to the UFC like no other," Ortiz continues. "I could have quit a long time ago, but there's no quit in me. I think about everything that I've done throughout my career, and it's been a really, really long road."

That road came to a close at the MGM Grand Garden Arena in Las Vegas in July of 2012. And though Ortiz lost his rubber match to Griffin at UFC 148, his fighting legacy is secure thanks to his reign atop the 205-pound weight class from 2000 to 2002 and his title fight wins over Wanderlei Silva, Yuki Kondo, Evan Tanner, Elvis Sinosic, Vladimir Matyushenko, and Shamrock.

"To be competing in the UFC for 15 years straight is something that I would have never imagined. I would have never imagined the success I've had here. I'm thankful for (UFC chairman and CEO) Lorenzo (Fertitta) and (UFC president) Dana (White) for giving me the opportunities that I've had in life. With hard work and dedication I was able to build my brand and build my career, and it's all thanks to the UFC."

PROFILE

WEIGHT CLASS: Light heavyweight
DATE OF BIRTH: 23 January, 1975
HEIGHT/WEIGHT: 6ft 3in, 205lb
BIRTHPLACE: Huntington Beach, CA
FIGHTING OUT OF: Huntington Beach, CA
STYLE: Submission Fighting
PROFESSIONAL MMA RECORD: 17-11-1

With his humor and self-effacing attitude, Forrest Griffin was the unlikeliest of mixed martial arts heroes, but by the time his career ended in 2013, he had won the first season of the groundbreaking Ultimate Fighter series, won a UFC light heavyweight championship, and engaged in some of the best fights the sport had ever seen against Stephan Bonnar, "Rampage" Jackson, and "Shogun" Rua. That's a legacy to be proud of.

But if you expected the 2013 inductee to the UFC Hall of Fame to retire with an emotional, tear-filled speech at UFC 160's post-fight press conference in May of 2013, then you don't know Griffin.

Then again, the original Ultimate Fighter winner and former UFC light heavyweight champion didn't endear himself to a generation of fight fans for his gravity in such situations.

"It's been a good eight years, I guess," Griffin deadpanned. "The biggest thing I've learned is that when (UFC president) Dana White says retire, you should retire. Otherwise you will blow your knee out before your next fight. Thank you guys."

With that, he walked off into the sunset after a career that not only entertained, but also helped put mixed martial arts on the mainstream map after his epic three round battle against Bonnar in the first TUF finale in April of 2005. Fittingly, White announced after the press conference that Griffin and Bonnar will go into the UFC Hall of Fame together.

And while Griffin kept it light in post-announcement statements, as is his custom, whenever he stepped into the Octagon for his 15 UFC fights, he was all business, a living example of the adage that while some fighters say they leave it all in there, he actually did it, beginning with the first fight against Bonnar, a three round slugfest that capped the first season of the reality show that saved the struggling UFC.

Eventually, Griffin proved that he belonged among the elite, eventually becoming a world champion. But the Octagon superstar never lost his sense of humor.

"I didn't get here through all that hard work and winning fights nonsense," he said. "I got here through a TV game show, and I'm comfortable with that."

He knew the real truth though, and through watching his work ethic and wins, so did we.

PROFILE

WEIGHT CLASS: Light heavyweight
DATE OF BIRTH: 16 March, 1979
HEIGHT/WEIGHT: 6ft 3in, 205lb
BIRTHPLACE: Columbus, OH
FIGHTING OUT OF: Las Vegas, NV
STYLE: Freestyle
PROFESSIONAL MMA RECORD: 19-7

One of the most beloved of competitors in UFC history, Forrest Griffin's career was filled with epic battles.

One-half of the most important match in UFC history against Forrest Griffin in 2005, Stephan Bonnar was no stranger to competing in big fights against the best of his era, as the hard-nosed battler took on everyone from Hall of Famers Griffin and Mark Coleman, to world champions Lyoto Machida, Rashad Evans, Jon Jones, and Anderson Silva over the course of a stellar 11 year career that endeared him to fight fans.

Inducted into the UFC Hall of Fame in July of 2013, Bonnar had retired at the age of 35 in October of 2012. Leaving the sport with a mark of 17-8, which included a final defeat at the hands of Silva at UFC 153, Bonnar's career will never be summed up as a collection of wins and losses, but more for what he brought to the Octagon night in and night out.

So to denigrate Bonnar for his defeats takes away what he did accomplish in the sport, the most important possibly being his first fight with Griffin in 2005, an epic three round battle that showed the rest of the world what the diehards knew about mixed martial arts. And it was something Bonnar knew was going to happen before the show that launched the sport, The Ultimate Fighter, even aired.

"I remember (UFC President) Dana White being worried that the show wasn't even gonna make it to TV, and I could tell he was worried that it wouldn't be a success," Bonnar said in 2009. "For some reason, in my mind, I was like 'what, are you kidding me? This thing's gonna be a hit and we're gonna have a bunch of seasons like this.' I always thought it was gonna be the coolest show ever."

Griffin-Bonnar I was certainly one of the coolest fights ever, as the two friendly rivals punched and kicked each other non-stop for three rounds, fighting as if more than a UFC contract was on the line. Griffin would emerge victorious that night, but both light heavyweights left the Cox Pavilion in Nevada with jobs, and it was just the next step for the almost accidental prizefighter dubbed "The American Psycho."

He was no mere brawler though, as the former Golden Gloves boxer also held a jiu-jitsu black belt under the late, great Carlson Gracie. But the standup wars made his reputation, marking him as one of the toughest and most exciting fighters of his era.

PROFILE

NAME: Stephan Bonnar
WEIGHT CLASS: Light heavyweight
DATE OF BIRTH: 4 April, 1977
HEIGHT/WEIGHT: 6ft 4in, 205lb
BIRTHPLACE: Munster, IN
FIGHTING OUT OF: Las Vegas, NV
STYLE: Boxing/Jiu-Jitsu/Taekwondo
PROFESSIONAL MMA RECORD: 17-8

UFC RECORDS

Since 1993, the UFC has captivated the world with the amazing performances of some of the greatest athletes to ever put on gloves. With an assist from FightMetric, here's the best of the best.

Most UFC Bouts

Tito Ortiz	27
Matt Hughes	25
Randy Couture	24
Chuck Liddell	23
Josh Koscheck	22
BJ Penn	22
Frank Mir	21
Chris Leben	21
Georges St-Pierre	20
Rich Franklin	20
Melvin Guillard	20
Chris Lytle	20

Most UFC Wins

Georges St-Pierre	18
Matt Hughes	18
Anderson Silva	16
Chuck Liddell	16
Randy Couture	16
Josh Koscheck	15
Tito Ortiz	15
Jon Fitch	14
Michael Bisping	14
Rich Franklin	14
Frank Mir	14

Most Consecutive Wins

Anderson Silva	16
Royce Gracie	11
Georges St-Pierre	11
Jon Jones	9
Junior dos Santos	9
Jon Fitch	8
Lyoto Machida	8
Gray Maynard	8
Chuck Liddell	7 (twice)
Ben Henderson	7
Jim Miller	7
Cain Velasquez	7
George Sotiropoulos	7
Randy Couture	7

Thiago Alves	7
Rich Franklin	7
Pat Miletich	7

##

Randy Couture	15
Georges St-Pierre	13
Anderson Silva	12
Matt Hughes	12
BJ Penn	11
Tito Ortiz	9
Tim Sylvia	9

Most Successful Title Defenses

Anderson Silva	10
Georges St-Pierre	8
Matt Hughes	5
Jon Jones	5
Jose Aldo	5
Tito Ortiz	5
Chuck Liddell	4
Frank Shamrock	4
Pat Miletich	4

Most Successful Consecutive Title Defenses

Anderson Silva	10
Georges St-Pierre	8
Matt Hughes	5
Jon Jones	5
Tito Ortiz	5
Jose Aldo	5
Chuck Liddell	4
Frank Shamrock	4
Pat Miletich	4

Most Championship Fights Won

Anderson Silva	11
Georges St-Pierre	11
Randy Couture	9
Matt Hughes	9
Jon Jones	6

Tito Ortiz	6
Jose Aldo	5
BJ Penn	5
Chuck Liddell	5
Frank Shamrock	5
Pat Miletich	5
Tim Sylvia	5

Most Championship Fights Lost

Randy Couture	6
Tim Sylvia	5
BJ Penn	5
Kenny Florian	3
Tito Ortiz	3
Matt Hughes	3

##

Georges St-Pierre	47
Randy Couture	44
BJ Penn	42
Frankie Edgar	34
Anderson Silva	31
Tito Ortiz	28
Matt Hughes	27

Most Knockouts in Championship Fights

Anderson Silva	7
Chuck Liddell	5
Randy Couture	5
Matt Hughes	5

Most Submissions in Championship Fights

Frank Shamrock	4
Matt Hughes	3
BJ Penn	3
Anderson Silva	2
Pat Miletich	2

Youngest Fighters to Compete in the UFC

Dan Lauzon	18
Vitor Belfort	19
Max Holloway	20
Robbie Lawler	20
Charles Oliveira	20
Michael McDonald	20
Nick Diaz	20
Thomas Egan	20
Rory MacDonald	20

Anderson Silva	17
Chuck Liddell	14
Melvin Guillard	13
Junior dos Santos	11
Lyoto Machida	11
Thiago Alves	10
Rich Franklin	10
Andrei Arlovski	8
Pat Barry	8
Yves Edwards	8
Jake Ellenberger	8
Quinton Jackson	8
Anthony Johnson	8
Nate Marquardt	8
Jorge Rivera	8
Wanderlei Silva	8
Georges St-Pierre	8
Cain Velasquez	8

Most Significant Strikes Landed

Georges St-Pierre	1153
Michael Bisping	947
Sam Stout	911
Frankie Edgar	908
BJ Penn	858
Rich Franklin	856
Chris Lytle	818
Forrest Griffin	796
Nate Diaz	768
Randy Couture	708

Best Significant Strike Accuracy

Anderson Silva	67.5%
Fabio Maldonado	63.5%
Evan Tanner	59.0%
Cheick Kongo	58.2%
Randy Couture	58.0%
Cain Velasquez	57.3%
Matt Brown	56.7%

Alex Caceres	56.5%
Lyoto Machida	56.0%
Fabricio Werdum	55.5%

Significant Strike Defense

Jon Madsen	81.4%
John Makdessi	76.2%
Georges St-Pierre	75.1%
Ryan Bader	72.4%
Jose Aldo	72.1%
Phil Davis	72.0%
Gray Maynard	71.9%
Frankie Edgar	71.4%
Max Holloway	71.3%
Rafael dos Anjos	70.7%

Total Strikes Landed

Georges St-Pierre	2,398
Jon Fitch	2,185
Chris Leben	1,780
BJ Penn	1,676
Nick Diaz	1,536
Chris Lytle	1,533
Chael Sonnen	1,394
Matthew Riddle	1,350
Nate Diaz	1,343
Randy Couture	1,337

Best Takedown Defense

Gleison Tibau	93.2%
Jose Aldo	89.7%
Andrei Arlovski	89.5%
Matthew Riddle	89.3%
Georges St-Pierre	88.0%
Gray Maynard	86.4%
Francis Carmont	85.7%
Rory MacDonald	85.7%
Yushin Okami	84.4%
Chuck Liddell	83.6%

Georges St-Pierre	84
Gleison Tibau	69
Jon Fitch	58
Karo Parisyan	53
Clay Guida	51
Sean Sherk	50
Rashad Evans	49
Randy Couture	46
Frankie Edgar	46
Nik Lentz	45

Shortest Average Fight Time

Drew McFedries	2:20
James Irvin	2:53
Frank Trigg	3:55
Houston Alexander	4:13
Ryan Jensen	4:15
Yoshiyuki Yoshida	4:15
Daniel Pineda	4:18
Erick Silva	4:23
John Albert	4:24
Ken Shamrock	4:34

Longest Average Fight Time

Benson Henderson	20:43
Demetrious Johnson	19:50
Jose Aldo	19:24
Frankie Edgar	18:05
Dan Henderson	16:02
Urijah Faber	15:43
Renan Barao	15:37
Sean Sherk	15:35
Georges St-Pierre	15:10
Riki Fukuda	15:00
Heath Herring	15:00
Diego Nunes	15:00
Michihiro Omigawa	15:00
Nam Phan	15:00

Rani Yahya	1.03
Pete Spratt	1.04
Ivan Salaverry	1.15
Phil Davis	1.16
Jon Madsen	1.18
Roan Carneiro	1.25
Renato Sobral	1.25
Chael Sonnen	1.26
Chad Mendes	1.27
Georges St-Pierre	1.27

Takedown Accuracy

Georges St-Pierre	75.0%
Nate Marquardt	73.0%
Jonathan Goulet	70.0%
Renato Sobral	66.7%
Chris Weidman	66.7%
Jamie Varner	65.6%
Lyoto Machida	65.0%
Rich Franklin	63.6%
Trevor Prangley	63.6%
Luigi Fioravanti	63.2%
Cheick Kongo	63.2%

All statistics correct to September 2013.

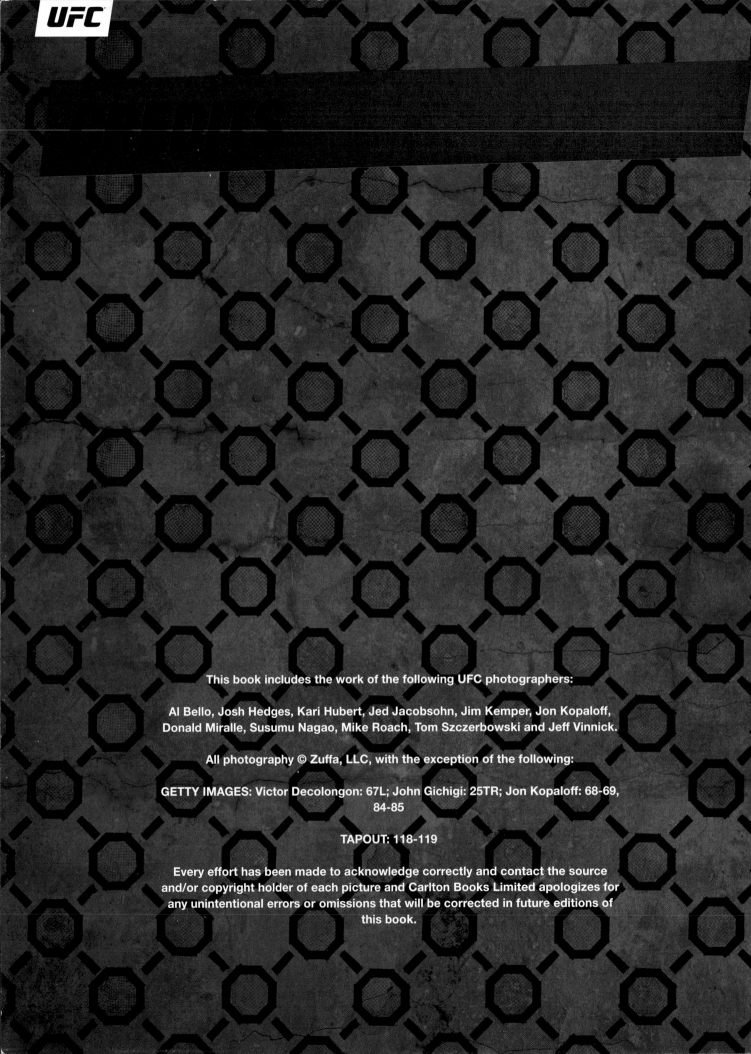

UFC